A Short Guide to Writing about Film

A Short Guide to Writing about Film

EIGHTH EDITION

TIMOTHY CORRIGAN
The University of Pennsylvania

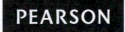

Boston   Columbus   Indianapolis   New York   San Francisco   Upper Saddle River
Amsterdam   Cape Town   Dubai   London   Madrid   Milan   Munich   Paris   Montreal   Toronto
Delhi   Mexico City   São Paulo   Sydney   Hong Kong   Seoul   Singapore   Taipei   Tokyo

Senior Sponsoring Editor: Virginia L. Blanford
Senior Marketing Manager: Sandra McGuire
Production Manager: Renata Butera
Creative Art Director: Jayne Conte
Cover Image: AVATAR, Zoe Saldana, 2009, TM & Copyright ©20th Century Fox.
  All rights reserved/Courtesy Everett Collection
Visual Researcher: Rona Tuccillo
Manufacturing Buyer: Renata Butera
Electronic Page Makeup: Integra Software Services Pvt. Ltd.
Printer and Binder: Edwards Brothers
Cover Printer: Lehigh-Phoneix Color/Hagerstown

Library of Congress Cataloging-in-Publication Data

Corrigan, Timothy.
  A short guide to writing about film / Timothy Corrigan. — 8th ed.
    p. cm.
Includes bibliographical references and indexes.
ISBN-13: 978-0-205-23639-8 (alk. paper)
ISBN-10: 0-205-23639-1 (alk. paper)
1. Film criticism. I. Title.
PN1995.C66 2012
808'.066791—dc22

                                    2011011760

1 2 3 4 5 6 7 8 9 10—EB—15 14 13 12 11

ISBN-13: 978-0-205-23639-8
ISBN-10:   0-205-23639-1

Contents

Preface

This book demonstrates—uniquely, I believe—how thinking about and writing about film are intricately bound together. Equally important, it draws on and develops the fact that students write better about a subject they know and like and that few subjects today are enjoyed and understood more universally than the movies. On the one hand, *A Short Guide to Writing about Film* walks students through the process of converting the fun and pleasure of watching a movie into the satisfaction of articulating ideas about that movie. With numerous student and professional examples along the way, it moves from note taking and first drafts to polished essays and research projects, demonstrating how an analysis of a film becomes more subtle and rigorous as part of a composition process. At the same time, the book assumes that we write better and more willingly about subjects with which we engage confidently and comfortably. For most students today, the movies are that subject, and *A Short Guide to Writing about Film* draws on that love and knowledge of films— ranging from movies that students easily recognize to ones they may only have read or heard about—as a way of encouraging and developing writing skills.

The aim of this book is threefold: to save time for instructors of film who, in presenting the complexities of the art and industry of film, are hard put to deal with the writing problems of students; to lessen students' anxiety about writing, by clarifying points that many instructors mistakenly presume students already know; and, in doing this, to encourage more enjoyable and articulate communication between the two.

UPDATES AND ENHANCEMENTS FOR THE EIGHTH EDITION

The challenge of a new edition of this book is that changes and additions must not, I believe, make the book become too cumbersome. In order to keep this book up-to-date and fresh, this eighth edition features seven prominent revisions:

- *New discussions of animation and 3-D technology.* There's no doubt that one of the more visible shifts in the cinema during the last ten years has been the growing presence and importance of

xi

animated films and, more recently, 3-D technology. While it's beyond the scope of this book to do complete justice to the impact of these two practices, the current edition has added discussions of both, featuring guidelines for how to critically consider both when writing about them.

- *Additional and revised resources for Internet research.* For the writer about film, the Internet has continued to grow as an important resource for reading, viewing, and research. Accordingly, these changing and expanding resources require continual updating, and this edition has edited and added to those sites where students can find good film journals, research links, and, for the first time in this book, sites where clips and complete films can be downloaded or streamed.

- *Expanded discussion of film narrative, sound, and adaptation.* The necessarily condensed discussions of film narrative, sound, and adaptation are three areas that students and reviewers suggested would benefit from some additional discussion. These new additions do not, needless to say, provide full and exhaustive accounts of the complexities of these three processes, but the fine-tuning has, I believe, made clearer the many ways a student might engage them as part of their critical thinking about film.

- *A new section of recommended books for further study.* Because this guide aims to both introduce students to film study and, ideally, motive them to continue to develop that interest, the book now includes a list of "further readings." This short, selective list includes excellent texts that expand the discussion of film analysis, film history, and film theory.

- *Revised exercises for students at the end of each chapter.* Whether they are regularly used or not, the short exercises at the end of each chapter remain popular with students and instructors, and the current edition has revised many of these to keep them fresh and effective.

- *Updated examples and illustrations of recent films.* A key adjustments in every new edition of this book has been integrating recent films into the discussions and illustrations. While I would insist that it's crucial to present older films or foreign films as a way of piquing students' curiosity and interest in films they may not (but should!) know, it is also paramount to provide examples of recent contemporary movies familiar to students. Ideally, this practice will engage students more in the discussion of central points and thus lead to better writing.

- *Silent films and early cinema.* This new version of the guide continues to attend to important films and filmmakers traditionally considered outside the historical mainstream. Here there has been particular attention to expanding the coverage of silent films and early cinema. While this book is clearly not a comprehensive history of film, it does aim to remind students of the vast array of materials, people, and topics available for writing good essays about film.

THE NEED FOR THIS BOOK

Those of us who teach film rarely have time to discuss writing about film. Most of us are busy presenting films and various books about those films, and the usual presumption we are forced to make is that students know how to put what they see and think into a comprehensible written form. As common and forgivable as that presumption may be, it is less reliable today than ever before. Instructors must increasingly puzzle over and bemoan those enthusiastic students who seem to know so much and are brimming with things to say about the movies but who write confused and disappointing papers.

One way to avoid this problem is to rely on examinations that elicit short answers. Yet as useful and as necessary as this method is, especially in large lecture courses on film history, it sidesteps several beneficial demands of the critical essay, demands that make real differences in the quality of a student's thinking. An essay forces a student to use special skills: to generate and focus original ideas; to organize, sustain, and support those ideas until they are fully developed; to fine-tune perceptions by revising the language used to describe them; to employ proper grammar and syntax as part of the convincing presentation of an argument; and to make use of the opinions of others through intelligent research.

Writing essays about films is, in short, one of the most sophisticated ways to respond to them. To elicit scope, originality, and rigor in a student's thinking, an instructor, I believe, needs to guide that student through the mechanics of the essay form. Filling the gap between writing handbooks and film-studies textbooks by distilling writing lessons as they apply specifically to film criticism, this book hopes to be that guide.

Although the emphasis is on the analytical writing done in most film courses, the book can be used in many ways, with a variety of other textbooks, and by any professor who believes that writing about film is part of learning about film. This is a concise and flexible book that can be adapted to a wide variety of writing courses or film courses as a supplemental or central text. In all cases, its goal is to promote good thinking and good writing about film.

ACKNOWLEDGMENTS

During the first stages of this book, Marcia Stubbs and Sylvan Barnet were consistently helpful and demanding in reading the manuscript and urging changes.

Since then, I am grateful to the many reviewers of the various editions, including Jeffrey Barlow, Pacific University; Austin Briggs, Hamilton College; Jim Collins, University of Notre Dame; David Cook, Emory University; Denise K. Cummings, University of Florida; Timothy Lyons, Emerson College; Jill R. Deans, Kansas State University; Pamela Demery, University of California, Davis; Cyndy Hendershot, Arkansas State University; Richard McGhee, Arkansas State University; Toby Miller, New York University; Betty Jo Peters, Morehead State University; Clay Reynolds, The University of Texas at Dallas; Deborah Rogers, University of Maine; James Schwoch, Northwestern University; Chuck Wasserburg, Northwestern University; Barbara Weitz, Florida International University; Emmett Winn, Auburn University; Tom Zaniello, Northern Kentucky University; Gus Amaya, Florida International University; Betty Bettacchi, Collin College; Wheeler Winston Dixon, University Nebraska, Lincoln; Tammy Kinsey, University of Toledo; Alexis Krasilovsky, California State University, Northridge; Kelli Marshall, Texas Christian University; John McGowan-Hartmann, University of New Orleans; and Shelley Rodrigo, Mesa Community College. In addition, the suggestions and advice of Lyn Tribble and Jeremy Butler have been indispensable in considering Internet research.

For the eighth edition, comments from the following reviewers have been of great help: Kimberly Nichele Brown, Texas A&M University; Kyle Edwards, Oakland University; Cynthia Riffe Hancock, University of North Carolina, Charlotte; Michael Rubinoff, Arizona State University; Lorraine K. Stock, University of Houston; and Brad Strickland, Gainesville State College.

I wish especially to thank—for their patience, assistance, and encouragement through our rich lives together since the inception of this book— Cecilia, Graham, and Anna Corrigan and, most of all, Marcia Ferguson.

TIMOTHY CORRIGAN

A Short Guide to Writing about Film

1

WRITING ABOUT THE MOVIES

WHY WRITE ABOUT THE MOVIES?

Commenting some years ago on his experience at the movies, the French writer Christian Metz described a challenge that still faces the student of movies today: We all understand the movies, but how do we explain them?

As a measure of that common understanding, notice the extent to which movies are a part of a cultural life that we generally take for granted. We all treasure and identify with certain movies—for their laughs, their thrills, or their haunting images of terror—and movies and their stars regularly become part of our daily lives and conversations. The 2010 release *The Social Network* dramatized a watershed moment in the Internet revolution, specifically as a tale about Mark Zuckerberg, the founder of Facebook. In 2009, Academy Award winner *The Hurt Locker* brought home to the United States the horror, pain, and confusion of the ongoing war in Iraq, while that same year *Avatar* brought home a war on alien planet with a 3-D technology that purportedly would revolutionize how we watch movies. In 2008, *The Dark Knight* set a record for an opening day with a $66.4 million gross, partly as a result of the tragic and much-publicized death of Heath Ledger, the actor who plays the Joker. In 1997, *Star Wars* lent its name to a controversial military project, and in 1991, *JFK* raised again unsettled questions about President John F. Kennedy's assassination that appeared on television and in newspapers for months before and after the movie's release. In a sense, Erwin Panofsky's 1934 words are probably truer today than ever before:

> If all the serious lyrical poets, composers, painters and sculptors were forced by law to stop their activities, a rather small fraction of the general public would become aware of the fact and a still smaller fraction would seriously regret it. If the same thing were to happen with the movies, the social consequences would be catastrophic. (234)

1

Publicly and privately, our lives have become so permeated by the movies that we rarely bother to think carefully about them—and less often, if at all, do we think of writing about them.

Normally, we might argue that there is little reason to struggle to explain—and certainly not in writing—what we understand primarily as entertainment. Whether in a movie theater or on late-night television, we usually watch films because we expect the kind of pleasure seldom associated with an inclination to pick up pen and paper. After seeing *Avatar* (2009), we might chat briefly about certain characters or scenes we particularly enjoyed or disliked, but we rarely want to offer a lengthy analysis of how the sets, the construction of the story, and the characters worked together. There is often an unspoken assumption that any kind of analysis might interfere with our enjoyment of the movies.

We are less reluctant to think analytically about other forms of entertainment. If, for instance, we watch a dance performance or a basketball game, we may easily and happily discuss some of their intricacies and complexities, realizing that our commentary adds to rather than subtracts from our enjoyment of them. At these times, our understanding of and pleasure in experiencing the event are products of the critical awareness that our discussion refines and elaborates on. The person who has no inclination or ability to reflect on or analyze basketball or dance may be entertained on some level, but the person who is able to activate a critical intelligence about the rules and possibilities involved experiences a richer kind of pleasure.

In fact, in these cases our ability to respond with some analytical awareness adds to our enjoyment. And not surprisingly, the same is true of our enjoyment of the movies. Informed audiences often turn to read a review of a show they have seen the night before; many of us enjoy reading about movies we have not even seen. Analytical thinking and reading about an "entertainment" invigorate and enrich it, and analytical writing about film offers the same promises and rewards. For example, when pressured to explain carefully why she liked *Avatar,* one student discovered that her understanding of and appreciation for the film were more complex and subtle than she had initially realized (Figure 1.01). Acknowledging that there was no missing the spectacular special effects of the film, she began to think more about not only what makes the film so enjoyable, but about how it communicates important ideas about humanity. She began her expanded response:

> While most discussions of the 2009 *Avatar* will undoubtedly focus on its revolutionary 3-D technology, we should not overlook the film's ability to skillfully tell a poignant, touching tale of human connection and integrity. As Jake (Sam Worthington) gradually

Figure 1.01 Writing about *Avatar* (2009) can become an opportunity to clarify and develop initial impressions into more developed ideas and thoughts about that film.

becomes aware of the imperialist aspirations and brutal goals of his corporate and political superiors, he undergoes a journey of personal discovery that leads to his eventual decision to side with the natives of the planet, the Na'vi. This journey takes place in lush extra-terrestrial fields and amidst the alien inhabitants of the planet Pandora, and audiences are transported–almost physically—to another world, one that has survived and flourished as a result of compassion and cooperation rather than greed and violence. The cold metallic nature of humanity's annexation of Pandora can be seen in their mining fields, guns, and bombs, while the Na'vi rely on the natural world, living in the trees and physically connecting with other indigenous species. At the center of the high-profile technology that made the film is, in short, an important message about a way of living that is both human and more than human.

If the movies inform many parts of our lives, we should be able to enjoy them in many ways, including the challenging pleasure of trying to think about, explain, and write about our experience watching them. We go to the movies for many reasons: to think or not to think, to stare at them, or to write about them. We may go to a movie to consume it like cotton candy; we may go to a film where that candy becomes food for the mind. As the fan of *Avatar* found out, analyzing our response to a movie does not ruin our enjoyment of it. Writing about a film can allow us to enjoy it (and other films) in ways we were incapable of before.

If watching and understanding is one of the pleasures of the movies, writing and explaining can be another exciting pleasure.

Let us keep in mind that writing about the movies is not so far from what most of us do already: When we leave a movie theater after two hours of enforced silence, most of us discuss or argue about the film. Although the difference between talking and writing about a subject is a crucial one, writing about a film is, in one sense, simply a more refined and measured kind of communication, this time with a reader. Our comments can be about the performance of an actor, the excitement elicited by specific scenes, or just common questions about what happened, why it happened, or why the film made the answers to these questions unclear.

Frequently, these conversations evolve from searching for the right word or finding a satisfactory description of how a sequence develops: "I prefer Keaton to Chaplin because Keaton's funnier. Well, I mean, he tells funnier, more complicated stories"; "I hated—no, I found much too predictable—the ending of *Inception* (2010)." While talking about movies, even very casually, we search for words to match what we saw and how we reacted to it. Writing about film is a careful and more calculated step beyond this first impulse to discuss what we have seen. Given this normal impulse, we can even enjoy talking and writing about a movie that we didn't like. A friend of the writer who praised *Avatar* thus begins his essay more negatively than the student quoted previously:

> While the 3-D technology of *Avatar* (2009) has pushed the current bounds of cinema to new levels, all the glitz and shiny aliens do nothing but rehash a plot already told hundreds of times before. The story—an invading soldier is reborn and accepted by those who were once his enemy—is engaging, but *Avatar's* heavy-handed messages of moral rectitude and the power of human understanding fall well short of its epic aspirations. The film's technology, rather than complementing the story, becomes the focal point of the entire movie and leaves little room for sufficient plot development. The long, yawning shots of the planet Pandora and its many natural wonders become more interesting than the story itself, leaving us waiting for the next 3-D object to pop out and wow the audience and resulting in a film that is little more than visual stimulation. *Avatar* seems convinced that its stunning use of 3-D technology would enamor viewers to the extent that no one would notice the clunky acting and lack of narrative subtlety. The stereotypical story of American invasion funded by corporate interests is a dull commonplace in contemporary movies, made even duller in *Avatar* by stock characters like a classically evil marine officer

and a spineless corporate representative. An unfortunately clumsy and unwieldy attempt at a simple, heartfelt concept, *Avatar* is, at best, an average, passable movie dressed up in shiny new clothes that never quite fit.

As these two friends discovered, when we understand the same movie very differently, trying to explain that understanding can be charged with all the energy of a good conversation.

Perhaps more than most other arts and entertainments, the movies frequently elicit a strong emotional or intellectual reaction. Often, however, the reason for our particular reaction to a movie remains unclear until we have had the opportunity to think carefully about and articulate what stimulated it. *Meet John Doe* (1941) might elicit a giddy nostalgia ridiculously out of step with today's political complexities; some viewers of *I Love You Phillip Morris* (2009) may find themselves attracted by the honest depiction of a gay relationship with depth and passion but be put off by Jim Carrey's typically exaggerated antics; most audiences of Fellini's *8 1/2* (1963) will probably recognize the importance of the opening sequence, in which a man floats from his car above a traffic jam, but they may be hard-pressed to explain quickly what it means in terms of the story that follows. Analyzing our reactions to themes, characters, or images like these can be a way not only of understanding a movie better, but also of understanding better how we view the world and the cultures we live in. In the following three paragraphs, we can see how Geoffrey Nowell-Smith turned his initial excitement about a scene in an Antonioni film into an exploration of that particular scene and, implicitly, into a discussion of his admiration of the human complexity in Antonioni's films:

> There is one brief scene in *L'Avventura*, not on the face of it a very important one, which seems to me to epitomize perfectly everything that is most valid and original about Antonioni's form of cinema. It is the scene where Sandro and Claudia arrive by chance at a small village somewhere in the interior of Sicily. The village is strangely quiet. They walk around for a bit, call out. No reply, nothing. Gradually it dawns on them that the village is utterly deserted, uninhabited, perhaps never was inhabited. There is no one in the whole village but themselves, together and alone. Disturbed, they start to move away. For a moment the film hovers: the world is, so to speak, suspended for two seconds, perhaps more. Then suddenly the film plunges, and we cut to a close-up of Sandro and Claudia making love in a field—one of the most ecstatic moments in the history of the cinema, and one for which there has been apparently no formal preparation whatever. What exactly has happened?

It is not the case that Sandro and Claudia have suddenly fallen in love, or suddenly discovered at that moment that they have been in love all along. Nor, at the other extreme, is theirs a panic reaction to a sudden fear of desolation and loneliness. Nor again is it a question of the man profiting from a moment of helplessness on the part of the woman in order to seduce her. Each of these explanations contains an aspect of the truth, but the whole truth is more complicated and ultimately escapes analysis. What precisely happened in that moment the spectator will never know, and it is doubtful if the characters really know for themselves. Claudia knows that Sandro is interested in her. By coming with him to the village she has already more or less committed herself, but the actual fatal decision is neither hers nor his. It comes, when it comes, impulsively: and its immediate cause, the stimulus which provokes the response, is the feeling of emptiness and need created by the sight of the deserted village. Just as her feelings (and his too for that matter) are neither purely romantic nor purely physical, so her choice, Antonioni is saying, is neither purely determined nor purely free. She chooses, certainly, but the significance of her choice escapes her, and in a sense also she could hardly have acted otherwise....

Where in this oppressive physical and social environment do the characters find any escape? How can they break out of the labyrinth which nature and other men and their own sensibilities have built up around them? Properly speaking there is no escape, nor should there be. Man is doomed to living in the world—this is to say no more than that he is doomed to exist. But the situation is not hopeless. There are moments of happiness in the films, which come, when they come, from being at peace with the physical environment, or with others, not in withdrawing from them. Claudia in *L'Avventura*, on the yacht and then on the island, is cut off, mentally, from the other people there, and gives herself over to undiluted enjoyment of her physical surroundings, until with Anna's disappearance even these surroundings seem to turn against her and aggravate rather than alleviate her pain. In *The Eclipse* Vittoria's happiest moment is during that miraculous scene at Verona when her sudden contentment seems to be distilled out of the simple sights and sounds of the airport: sun, the wind in the grass, the drone of an aeroplane, a jukebox. At such moments other people are only a drag—and yet the need for them exists. The desire to get away from oneself, away from other people, and the satisfaction this gives, arise only from the practical necessity for most of the time of being aware of oneself and of forming casual or durable relationships with other people. And the relationships too can be a source of fulfillment. No single trite or abstract formulation can catch the living essence of Antonioni's version of the human comedy. (355, 363)

In this example, a single scene becomes the stimulus for the essay. The author probes and questions this scene: What exactly has happened, and what does it mean? His obvious satisfaction as a writer comes from analyzing this scene as if it were a mystery to be solved. In the process of his analysis, his original curiosity leads to broader readings of other Antonioni movies and, finally, to his discovery of a consolation in the disturbing predicament that first caught his eye. For this writer, the pleasure of following his curiosity leads to the larger pleasure of understanding more about life and happiness in modern times.

YOUR AUDIENCE AND THE AIMS OF FILM CRITICISM

Writing about film can serve one of several functions. It can help you do the following:

- Understand your own response to a movie better
- Convince others why you like or dislike a film
- Explain or introduce something about a movie, a filmmaker, or a group of movies that your readers may not know
- Make comparisons and contrasts between one movie and others as a way of understanding them better
- Make connections between a movie and other areas of culture to illuminate both the culture and the movies it produces

The purposes that become part of or central to your writing will sometimes depend entirely on your audience: An essay introducing a new movie, for example, is usually written for an audience that has not seen the film. However, even when that purpose is decided on independently—perhaps out of a personal interest in the relation between Spanish films and Spanish culture—what you say will always be shaped by your notion of your audience and especially by what you presume those readers know or want to know.

If you think of writing as, in some ways, resembling conversation, you will see how the notion of an audience helps shape what you say. If, for example, you are discussing an American movie, such as *The Blind Side* (2009), with a non-American, both the way you make your point about the film and, perhaps, the point itself will be determined by what you believe that individual knows and wants to know about American culture and about the movie. (A non-American, for example, may need more information about American football and college recruitment of high-school players, while an American will need very little information.) Similarly, in

discussing a film with someone who may not have seen it, I would probably first describe that film with a general overview, summarizing the plot
and themes as a way to convince that person to see the film or not to see
it. If, on the other hand, I am talking about a movie that a friend and I
have both seen several times, such as *Slumdog Millioniare* (2008), I do not
have to remind that person of the plot or of the main characters. Just as
our conversations about movies differ according to the individuals we are
speaking with, the way we write about film and even the critical position
we choose vary depending on the audience we are writing for.

One schematic and traditional way to indicate the different audiences
a writer might envision is to distinguish among the following:

- A screening report
- A movie review
- A theoretical essay
- A critical essay

A great deal of writing about film today now appears on the Internet,
and this kind of open forum does tend to blur these distinctions, just as it
blurs a clear sense of the intended audience for different kinds of writing.
While these four modes of writing are hardly exhaustive or completely
distinct, they should indicate the importance of keeping your audience in
mind as a way of determining your style and goals.

The Screening Report

A screening report is a short piece of writing that acts as a preparation
for class discussions and examinations. Primarily a descriptive assignment
that organizes notes on a film (see pp. 23–25), the report should contain
about three or four paragraphs (about one to two pages) focused on two
to four points related to the topics of the course or to specific questions
provided by the instructor (your target audience for this kind of writing).
Unlike a review or critical essay, a screening report avoids strong opinions
or a particular argument. Instead, it aims to be as objective and concrete
as possible, including audio and visual detail wherever possible. For a class
on the road movie, one student begins his screening report of Terrence
Malick's *Badlands* (1973) this way:

> 1. *Badlands* as Road Movie: Narrative. Characteristic of this genre
> is the journey away from home and onto an open road. Like other
> road movies, here there are no apparent goals, except flight, and the
> plot develops as a series of episodic events and encounters. After the
> murder of Holly's father, she and Kit almost randomly kill people they

encounter on the road, as a kind of parody of the violence found in other road movies.

    2. *Badlands* and the Road Movie: Compositions. The most obvious emblem of a road movie is the moving perspective of the car that carries Kit and Holly along the open roads of the West. The framing of numerous shots in this film call attention to the vast and empty spaces that surround the characters, but unlike more realistic road movies, the luminous images of *Badlands* often create surreal landscapes. The sound track is an unusual variation on the genre: Holly's voice-over narration makes the story seem like a cheap romantic novel, and the music ranges from the operatic to honky-tonk.

Since this is a first sketch of the report, more specific details must be added later. Precise description of several shots and scenes will then provide compelling support for discussions in class and for preparation for examinations.

The Movie Review

The movie review is the type of film analysis with which most of us are chiefly familiar, since it appears in almost every newspaper. Normally, a review aims at the broadest possible audience, the general public with no special knowledge of film. Accordingly, its function is to introduce unknown films and to recommend or not recommend them. Because it presumes that an audience has not seen the movie it discusses, much of the essay is devoted to summarizing the plot or placing the film in another context (the director's other work, films of the same genre, and so on) that might help the reader understand it. Here, Vincent Canby's review introduces the readers of the *New York Times* to Malick's *Badlands* (1973):

> In Terrence Malick's cool, sometimes brilliant, always ferociously American film, "Badlands," which marks Malick's debut as a director, Kit and Holly take an all-American joyride across the upper Middle West, at the end of which more than half a dozen people have been shot to death by Kit, usually at point blank range. "Badlands" is the first feature by Mr. Malick, a 29-year-old former Rhodes Scholar and philosophy student whose only other film credit is as the author of the screenplay for the nicely idiosyncratic "Pocket Money." "Badlands" was inspired by the short, bloody saga of Charles Starkweather who, at age 19, in January, 1958, with the apparent cooperation of his 14-year-old girlfriend, Carol Fugate, went off on a murder spree that resulted in 10 victims. Starkweather was later executed in the electric chair and Miss Fugate given life imprisonment.

"Badlands" inevitably invites comparisons with three other important American films—Arthur Penn's "Bonnie and Clyde" and Fritz Lang's "Fury" and "You Only Live Once"—but it has a very different vision of violence and death. Mr. Malick spends no great amount of time invoking Freud to explain the behavior of Kit and Holly, nor is there any Depression to be held ultimately responsible. Society is, if anything, benign....

"Badlands" is narrated by Holly in the flat, nasal accents of the Middle West and in the syntax of a story in *True Romances.* "Little did I realize," she tells us at the beginning of the film, "that what began in the alleys and by-ways of this small town would end in the Badlands of Montana." At the end, after half a dozen murders, she resolves never again to "tag around with the hell-bent type."

Kit and Holly share with Bonnie and Clyde a fascination with their own press coverage, with their overnight fame ("The whole world was looking for us," says Holly, "for who knew where Kit would strike next?"), but a lack of passion differentiates them from the gaudy desperados of the thirties. Toward the end of their joyride, the bored Holly tells us she passed the time, as she sat in the front seat beside Kit, spelling out complete sentences with her tongue on the roof of her mouth.

Mr. Malick tries not to romanticize his killers, and he is successful except for one sequence in which Kit and Holly hide out in a tree house as elaborate as anything the MGM art department ever designed for Tarzan and Jane. Mr. Sheen and Miss Spacek are splendid as the self-absorbed, cruel, possibly psychotic children of our time, as are the members of the supporting cast, including Warren Oates as Holly's father.

One may legitimately debate the validity of Mr. Malick's vision, but not, I think, his immense talent. "Badlands" is a most important and exciting film. (40)

We can identify more than one function in this essay. Canby aims to convince his reader that *Badlands* is an important movie that is worth seeing, and he does this by introducing Malick and his credentials, by describing the plot and the historical background of that plot, by evaluating the acting, and by placing Malick's movie in the context of other films like it (specifically, *Bonnie and Clyde* [1967] and the two Fritz Lang movies). Equally important, however, is his clear sense of his audience: readers who probably know the popular *Bonnie and Clyde* but little about Malick and the background of *Badlands.* These are readers who have not yet seen the film and would like to know the outline of the story and a little about the characters and actors (Figure 1.02).

Figure 1.02 Like most films, *Badlands* (1973) provokes a variety of ways to think and write about it: screening reports, reviews, critical essays, and theoretical reflections.

The Theoretical Essay

The more theoretical essay—for instance, an essay on the relation of film and reality, on the political or ideological foundations of the movie industry, or on how film narrative is unlike literary narrative—is at the other end of the spectrum. Such an essay often supposes that the reader possesses a great deal of knowledge about specific films, film history, and other writings about film. Its target audience, often advanced students or people who teach film studies, is usually very knowledgeable about the movies. Perhaps arguing what is unique about cinematic representation or perhaps showing what the cinema shares with other arts, a film essay that is primarily theoretical offers an explanatory model that illuminate more than one film, aiming to explain some of the larger and more complex structures of the cinema and how we understand them. Note the changes in style, choice of words, and assumptions about the reader's knowledge that point to this writer's 1953 conception of her audience:

> Here is new art. For a few decades it seemed like nothing more than a new technical device in the sphere of drama, a new way of preserving and retailing dramatic performances. But today its development has already belied this assumption. The screen is not a stage, and what is created in the conception and realization of a film is not a play. It is too early to

systematize any theory of this new art, but even in its present pristine state
it exhibits quite beyond any doubt, I think—not only a new technique, but
a new poetic mode. (Langer 411)

Whereas Canby could use expressions suitable to a review, such as
"gaudy desperados," "all-American joyride," and "important and exciting
film," the phrases might seem out of place in an essay by the philoso-
pher Susanne Langer. It is not that one style is more correct than the
other; it is simply a question of audience. A novice to film studies might
feel somewhat lost in Langer's comparatively accessible essay on film
theory. The reason is that novices are not the audience that this writer
supposes; she imagines an audience with experience in the study of history,
aesthetics, and philosophy and some understanding of the debates about
stage drama versus movies. The purpose of her essay is not difficult to see
(to convince her readers of the significance of film as an art), but how she
argues her point is understandable when we realize that she is addressing
an academic and intellectual community that, at the time, was suspicious
of the status of the movies as an art.

The Critical Essay

The critical essay usually expected in film courses falls between the
theoretical essay and the movie review. The writer of this kind of essay
presumes that his or her reader has seen or is at least familiar with the
film under discussion, although that reader may not have thought exten-
sively about it. This writer might therefore remind the reader of key
themes and elements of the plot, but a lengthy retelling of the story of
the film is neither needed nor acceptable. The focus of the essay is far
more specific than that of a review, because the writer hopes to reveal
subtleties or complexities that may have escaped viewers on the first or
even the second viewing. Thus the essay might focus on a short sequence
at the beginning of the film or on a camera angle that becomes associated
with a specific character. In the following excerpt, Brian Henderson also
discusses *Badlands*, but whereas Canby's audience was the reader of a
large newspaper, Henderson's audience is more academic, similar to the
one a student might address in a film course:

> Whatever their wishes, critics of Terrence Malick's *Badlands* (1973)
> have been drawn into polemical dispute. Writers favorable to the
> film have defended it against those who called it a failure when it first
> appeared and against those who have ignored it since then. The issue
> has been further complicated, and polemics renewed, by the release in
> 1978 of Malick's *Days of Heaven*.

This is not a favorable background for the serious criticism of any work, still less for that open-ended exploration which a new and unstudied work invites. I believe *Badlands* is one of the most remarkable American films of the 1970s, but I have no interest here in addressing the arguments against it. I assume, at any rate, that the film will be seen and studied for a long time to come.

What is attempted here is a beginning analysis of *Badlands*, or perhaps several beginnings. I take an obvious point of departure: the film's voiceover narration by Holly—indeed only its first part, approximately the film's first sixteen minutes. This is, emphatically, just one approach to the film and not a privileged one. A consideration of Holly's narration opens up other topics and leads to other analyses, but any approach does this.

To treat Holly's narration as I wish to do it is necessary to say something in advance about the film's dramaturgy, acting style and use of language. These important topics deserve, needless to say, fuller treatment than my prefatory remarks provide.

Badlands' approach to character is undeniably modern. Kit and Holly are both blank and not blank, emotionless and filled with emotion, oblivious to their fates and caught up in them, committed to the trivial but aware—glancingly—of the essential. They are empty, hence constantly fill themselves up with useless objects, souvenirs, movie-magazine gossip; they pose tests for themselves and try on different make-up, clothes, attitudes, roles. This is an "existential" view of character, and it undoubtedly leads to contradictions by conventional standards. Thus Kit and Holly are in love, living only for the moments they spend together; but they play cards with boredom in the country and even find sex boring. Holly kids with her father and (almost) weeps when he dies, but runs away with his killer a few hours later....

Every mode of cinema has a mode of dramaturgy distinctive to it and a corresponding distinctive acting or performance style. *Badlands*, which may represent a cinematic mode in and of itself, requires a special kind of acting to take its place within, but not upset, a very delicate balance of mise-en-scène, narrative, voiceover, music, etc. We must be able to look at Kit and Holly and to look through them sometimes alternately, sometimes simultaneously. This requires an acting style at once flat and flamboyant, realistic and theatrical. Our eyes must be on the characters even as we are paying attention to other things. Our attention is continually drawn toward the characters, and distracted away from them. Sheen and Spacek realize these requirements superbly, filling the film with their interesting sounds and motions

but never resolving into anything, never substantializing, defining or
"becoming" characters. Perhaps more correctly, their series of poses
is readable as exactly that, or as eccentric character. As in Brecht, it
is difficult to distinguish the acting style of the performers from the
nature of the characters. (38–40)

Canby and Henderson's essays are both positive responses to
Badlands, and they share similar interests. They differ significantly,
however, in aim and audience. At least as Henderson declares it, the
purpose of his essay is not so much to convince his readers to like or
dislike the film but to add to their understanding of it. He assumes that
his readers will continue to see and study the movie and, perhaps, to
add to the academic debate about it. He also takes for granted that his
audience knows the story, knows the characters, and is familiar with
terms like *mise-en-scène;* accordingly, he can choose very specific parts
of the film—Holly's narration and the acting style—to demonstrate his
point that there are important innovations in *Badlands.* Finally, even in
this section of the essay, one sees an organization typical of a good critical
argument: The writer begins by placing the film in the context of other
critical and scholarly views, announces his aim, and then moves from an
analysis of character and acting style to some general conclusions about
how to understand this style.

For the student writer, the question of audience, highlighted in
these three essays, is equally central to writing about film. Sometimes,
an instructor may give you an assignment aimed at a specific audience
and testing your ability to address that audience: "Write a review of
A Serious Man (2009) for the readers of *Time* magazine." More often,
your instructor will simply ask you to write a critical essay. Keep in
mind that your audience in these cases is neither your instructor alone
(who, you might imagine, can learn nothing from you) nor some large
and unknown public in the streets (to whom you might be prone to
tell the most obvious facts about a movie). Rather, envision your audience in most situations as your fellow students, individuals who have
seen the movie and may know something about it but who have not
studied it closely. This audience will probably not need to be told that
"*The Wizard of Oz* is an old American film that has become a children's
classic"; they may, however, be interested if you note that "*The Wizard
of Oz* was directed by Victor Fleming, who the same year (1939) made
Gone with the Wind." Likewise, few of your fellow viewers need to be
told that "Ophul's *The Sorrow and the Pity* (1970) is a very long French
movie about World War II," but they may be fascinated by a detailed
description of the opening shots.

Opinion and Evaluation

When you write about film, personal opinion and taste will necessarily become part of your argument. Some critics, for example, have a conscious or unconscious prejudice against foreign films. Others favor the work of a single director, such as John Huston or Wes Anderson. Still others, annoyed by literary adaptations unless they are faithful to the original, dislike films such as the contemporary version of Shakespeare's *Othello* called *O* (2001) but defend the Shakespeare films of Kenneth Branagh. Even those essays that appear to be chiefly descriptive or analytical—biographical or historical writings or essays that aim at an objective analysis of a sequence of shots—involve a certain amount of personal choice and evaluation. In some essays, factual description may be more prominent than evaluative judgments, but the differences are of degree, not kind. Most writing about film involves some personal opinion and evaluation.

No reader, of course, will be satisfied with a writer who uses his personal opinions to avoid or disguise a solid critical position. After watching Laurence Olivier's adaptation of Shakespeare's *Henry V* (1944), one student wrote,

> Although I have not read that many Shakespeare plays, this is the first one I ever liked. The opening, I think, is the most interesting part and the section that first grabbed my attention, because, in my opinion, it literally transforms what I feel is a dry play into an exciting film and, at the same time, comments on the difference between drama and film. In those opening images, it seems to me that Olivier acknowledges the original stage world of the drama and shows, I feel, how the movies can transcend dramatic limits. He makes the play much more alive for me.

Here the excess of *I*'s and personal qualifiers weakens the point the writer wishes to make, and it is doubtful that idiosyncratic problems, such as the writer's limited experience with the Shakespeare plays, are of the faintest interest to any reader. However, removing all references to the writer's personal experience of the film results only in stiffer but equally unsure prose:

> The opening is the most interesting part of *Henry V* (1944), because it comments on the central difference between drama and film. In these opening images, Olivier acknowledges the original stage world of the drama and shows how the movies can transcend those dramatic limits.

Somewhere in between, the writer finds the proper balance of personal experience and objective observation, judiciously integrating those personal experiences and feelings about the film that are probably also valid for other viewers:

> Even for the viewer uneasy with a Shakespeare play, Olivier's *Henry V* (1944) is an engaging experience. For me, the opening is the most interesting part and the section which is most likely to attract a reluctant viewer, because it literally transforms what, for some, might be a dry play into an expansive film and, at the same time, comments on the central difference between drama and film. In these opening images, Olivier acknowledges the original stage world of the drama and shows how the movies can transcend those dramatic limits. For viewers like myself, Shakespeare suddenly comes alive.

The useful rule of thumb here is to try to be aware of when and how your personal perspective and feelings enter your criticism and to what degree they are valuable or not—when, in short, those judgments seem to say something true not only for yourself, but for others, as well. A personal distaste for action films or, say, for slow-paced romantic stories could become a rich part of an essay when the writer carefully thinks through and offers reasons for that distaste. Or my expectations, as someone who mainly sees slick Hollywood films, could be crucial in analyzing my slight confusion yet fascination with a film by the Mexican filmmaker Guillermo del Toro—such as *Pan's Labyrinth* (2006)—because other viewers have often shared that confusion.

In the examples used earlier, both Canby and Henderson openly introduce their own opinions and personalities into their argument. Neither balks at using *I* to underline the presence of his perspective: "One may legitimately debate the validity of Mr. Malick's movie, but not, I think, his immense talent" (Canby); "I take an obvious point of departure: the film's voiceover narration by Holly.... This is, emphatically, just one approach to the film and not a privileged one" (Henderson). Canby's is perhaps a more opinionated *I;* Henderson's is more detached and cautious. Yet both Canby and Henderson use their personal positions to help form and energize their different responses to Malick's film. One might say that these uses of *I* are only the most forthright and direct indication of the many other evaluations and judgments that enter the essays: Canby's criticism of the romantic, junglelike setting where the two outlaws hide and Henderson's interest in narrative and theoretical questions about "performance."

When you write about the movies, personal feelings, expectations, and reactions may be the beginning of an intelligent critique, but they must be balanced with rigorous reflection on where those feelings and expectations and reactions come from and how they relate to more objective factors concerning the movie in question: its place in film history, its cultural background, and its formal strategies. François Truffaut, both an intelligent filmmaker and a perceptive critic, has observed that "instead of indulging passions in criticism, one must at least try to be critical with some purpose…. What is interesting is not pronouncing a film good or bad, but explaining why" (370).

Writing about film, then, is admittedly complex. It can also be exciting and rewarding. In 1908, Leo Tolstoy remarked about the movies, "You can see that this little clicking contraption with the revolving handle will make a revolution in our life—in the life of writers" (410). Try to approach films with the same interest and shrewdness. Try to conceive of yourself as a writer with an equally purposeful and dynamic relationship with the movies you watch and enjoy. Or, in the words of filmmaker Sally Potter, director of *Thriller* (1979), *Orlando* (1992), *The Tango Lesson* (1997), and *Rage* (2009), remember that there is a "pleasure in analysis, in unravelling, in thinking" (Pam Cook 27).

Exercises

1. Take opposite sides in a debate about a single film. Write one paragraph criticizing the film and then one paragraph defending it. In both cases, focus on a single scene to make your point.
2. Write a screening report on a film and then a review of three or four paragraphs. Then rewrite the review as a critical essay. Explain briefly the audiences you envisioned, the main differences in each piece of writing, and what is gained and lost in each.

2

BEGINNING TO THINK, PREPARING TO WATCH, AND STARTING TO WRITE

Of the several difficulties in writing about film, one of the most prominent is getting a handle on an experience that has so many different layers. Put simply, what should you choose to analyze and to write about? The story? The acting? The editing? Watching a film involves everything from the place where we see it and the price we pay to the size of the screen, the pace of the story, and the kind of music used as the background for that story. In Jean Cocteau's words, "The cinema muse is too rich." As the first step to an intelligent viewing, spectators need to break the habit of watching films "out of the corners of their eyes," as Cocteau puts it (217). This is where analysis begins.

Certainly our primary experience of a movie is the singular and, perhaps, private one of watching it for the first time—involved and enjoying it, one hopes, but possibly annoyed yet still somewhat involved. As the director in Jean-Luc Godard's 1983 film *First Name: Carmen* (played by Godard himself) writes, "Badly seen, badly said": Seeing a movie with all your attention is the only way to begin writing about a film—even one you don't like. Either as preparation before the screening or shortly afterward, however, you, as the writer, need to sort out that personal and primary experience along manageable lines, and this sorting out should become the groundwork for your analysis of the movie. Should you talk about the characters? About technological innovations? About the film's effect on an audience? Where should you start to direct your attention and your analysis so that you do not give yourself the impossible task of writing about the whole movie? Because the movies you see on the screen are a product of many different forces—writers, production demands, the cost of technology, and hundreds of others—that in a sense precede the images you are watching, it is necessary to approach those movies with sensitivity to some of these basic questions, influences, and problems. In the movies, much energy and time go into "preproduction" activity, when directors and producers outline and prepare scripts and filming strategies; your analysis will be better if you similarly spend at least some time on general, preliminary questions. As far as possible, prepare yourself for a movie; even before it starts, ask questions about it and about your own potential interest in it:

1. As an art form, the movies involve literature, the pictorial and plastic arts, music, dance, theater, and even architecture. The student interested in architecture might thus respond keenly to an Eisenstein or Antonioni movie if he or she can direct that interest to how these filmmakers use architectural space to add to the drama they are presenting. A music or art student might be drawn to certain art or experimental films, such as *Berlin: Symphony of a City* (1927), or to the musical or artistic features of a movie (Figure 2.01). Ask yourself which art forms interest you most and which you know the most about. Could you use your knowledge of literature or painting as a guide to a particular film? What might be behind the large number of recent adaptations of famous novels, like Mira Nair's version of a William Thackeray novel, *Vanity Fair* (2004), or the Cohen brothers' adaptation of Cormac McCarthy's *The Road* (2009)? Might your interest in popular or classical music suggest that you look for a topic in movies like *Holiday Inn* (1942), *West Side Story* (1961), *Moulin Rouge!* (2001), or *Sweeney Todd* (2007)?

Figure 2.01 Kenji Mizoguchi's *Utamaro and His Five Women* (1946) tells the tale of one of Japan's most renowned visual artists. His celebrity rests on the brilliant *ukiyo-e* wood-block prints he produced in the early nineteenth century, and Mizoguchi's cinematic recreation of that life raises many questions for the student of art: For instance, is there a connection here between the popular art of the movies and the popular art of *ukiyo-e* prints? Does the film recreate certain techniques or features of that artistic tradition?

2. The film industry depends on and responds quickly to changes in technology. Having grown used to contemporary Hollywood movies, most of us find that we react differently to a silent movie or to one in black and white—an obvious example of how the early technology that produced these movies determines how we view them. Many other tools of the trade—various sound technologies, color stocks, or special effects—can likewise become the starting point for a revealing analysis. Whether a movie is made for a large screen or for a television screen can say a great deal about the story (note how epic movies like *The Ten Commandments* [1956] just don't seem the same on television). As some commentators have suggested, the computer technology used in *The Matrix* (1999) may be the most interesting topic concerning that movie. If you are interested in technology, prepare to note features of the movie and its story that might depend on technology. Does the director make special use of black-and-white film stocks? Why? Does sound technology seem to play a large part in the movie? Is the movement (or lack of movement) of the camera related to the kind of camera used (like the handheld cameras of the French New Wave, which conveyed a sense of on-the-spot realism)? Especially in recent years, what is known as "digital convergence" has had an increasing impact on the film industry: More and more films are shot with digital cameras; the majority of movies are now edited with digital nonlinear editing programs (see pp. 68–69); computer-generated images have allowed filmmakers to not only add to the shape and colors of recorded realities, but also to create entirely new realities; and, finally, the distribution and exhibition of movies across the Internet and through handheld devices promises to change dramatically the way we see and understand films. Ask yourself how exactly this latest technological revolution can be seen in certain movies. Has digitalization altered how film characters are portrayed? How stories are constructed? What seems realistic or not? Pursuing these and other initial questions will usually require some later research and thinking to be answered adequately and to become related to an analysis of the movie. The student with some initial interest in the industrial and technological side of the movies, however, will often find good material for a strong essay if he or she approaches movies on the lookout for the role technology plays in them.

3. Film technology, production, and distribution are commercial and economic enterprises. It is crucial to keep this in mind when approaching any movie. If, for instance, a viewer is going to see a low-budget independent film (such as Michael Snow's *Wavelength* [1967]) at the local art house, the expectations about that movie will—and should—be different from those about a glossy blockbuster with a budget over $100 million

(such as Ridley Scott's *Robin Hood* [2010]) at a showcase cinema. No film is necessarily good or bad because of its commercial or economic constraints and freedoms, but the ability to adjust one's expectations does allow a viewer to more accurately assess the achievements or failures of a movie. Thus, for some films from South America or Africa, the often rough and unpolished look is not only an unavoidable by-product of financial constraints but, in some cases, also a conscious political sign used to distinguish them from the glossy products of Hollywood. At the other end of the economic scale are the massive Hollywood productions, with gargantuan budgets that mean they must capture the largest possible audience and so must take very few risks that might alienate part of that audience. Although this sort of angle on a movie will require some research if it is to develop into an essay, an awareness of or sensitivity to the economic and commercial determinants behind any movie can prepare you for a more intelligent and complex response to the images on the screen. Be open-minded and suspicious: If it looks like a movie that was made inexpensively, does this reduced cost allow it to do and say things that a big-budget movie might not be able to? Conversely, how do some Hollywood movies take advantage of a big budget or make creative use of a small budget? Where is much of the money directed? The stars? The special effects? The promotion? Why? Does the film seem especially earthy or commercial, or does it try to reach a compromise between the two? Why? Who is the intended audience for the film? Teenagers? The middle class? Intellectuals? Men? Women?

Having these and other preparatory questions in mind as you sit down to watch a movie will sharpen and direct your analytical abilities. These questions can be a crucial guide through a first viewing, that difficult time when you are trying to determine what is worth writing about and what is not. After seeing D. W. Griffith's *The Birth of a Nation* (1915) for the first time, one student dismissed it as a "primitive and racist story with a lot of old-fashioned images"; another student simply accepted it as "almost a documentary about the Civil War and the Reconstruction." David Cook's analysis, however, is influenced by a sense of the historical complications and limitations of the movie, as well as a sense of the presumptions of a modern audience watching it many years later:

> In its monumental scale, in its concentration upon a crucial moment in American history, in its mixture of historical and invented characters, in its constant narrative movement between the epochal and the human, and, most significantly, in its chillingly accurate vision of an American society predicated on race, *The Birth of a Nation* is a profoundly

American epic. We can fault Griffith for badly distorting the historical facts of Reconstruction, for unconscionably stereotyping the African-American as either fool or brute, and for glorifying a terrorist organization like the Klan, but we cannot quarrel with his basic assumption that American society was, and is, profoundly racist. That he endorses and encourages this situation rather than condemns it is properly repellent to contemporary audiences, as it was to many persons in 1915. But we must not allow our sympathies to obscure our own critical judgment, for then we make the same mistake as Griffith. And, as Americans, we must never overlook the possibility that the impetus for our most hostile reactions to Griffith's racism lies somewhere within our most deeply cherished illusions about ourselves. (79)

Like Cook, a curious and perceptive student might even follow up this thinking about race, Griffith's film, and its historical context by investigating a very different response to those questions and issues at that time. Most notably, African American filmmaker Oscar Micheaux's 1920 *Within Our Gates* assumes a very different audience, has fewer technological and economic resources, and presents a massively different view of race relations in the early twentieth century, and the result is a film that provokes its own set of compelling questions for the perceptive writer.

SUBJECT MATTER AND MEANING

The previously mentioned preliminary questions should remind you that the images you see are the product of certain influences and conditions, not just the world seen through a frame. The movies are not just about a subject but the rendition of that subject for particular reasons and to create certain meanings. Films are not just about a story, a character, a place, or a way of life; they are also what John Berger has called "a way of seeing" these elements in our lives. Any film at any point in history might describe a family, a war, or the conflict between races, but the ways these are shown and the reasons they are shown in a particular way can vary greatly. These variations, through which a subject is given a specific meaning or meanings, are a large part of what analysis is concerned with. Why does the student who dismissed *The Birth of a Nation* later hail *Black Hawk Down* (2001), another film about a war involving races, as "one of the best movies ever made"? The subject is roughly similar, but the meaning has changed significantly for that student.

To write an intelligent, perceptive analysis of the stories and characters in the movies, you must be prepared to see them as constructed according to certain forms and styles that arise from many different historical influences. This is what analysis of the movies is fundamentally about: examining how a subject has been formed to mean something specific through the power of art, technology, and commerce. Be prepared to respond to the influences that most interest you. Be prepared with a questioning mind from the beginning.

SILENT DIALOGUE: TALKING BACK TO THE MOVIES

Once the movie starts, your preliminary questions should become more and more specific regarding the movie you are watching, what it is about, and how it is constructed.

One of the most helpful techniques in preparing to write analytically about literature is our scribbling of marginal comments next to a text, the underlining we do, or simply the question marks we put next to difficult passages. No one approaches a book or work of art with all the answers or even all the questions. Part of the excitement in viewing or reading a challenging work comes from the questions it provokes. Thomas De Quincey's "On the Knocking at the Gate in *Macbeth*" originates in a specific question that De Quincey asked himself after seeing a production of the play: "From my boyish days I had always felt a great perplexity on one point in *Macbeth*. It was this: The knocking at the gate which succeeds to the murder of Duncan produced to my feeling an effect for which I never could account" (389). What, he asked himself, produced that effect? From that very specific question and personal uncertainty came one of the best essays ever written on Shakespeare.

This kind of questioning and annotating is one of the surest ways to start an analysis of a movie. In contrast to literature, however, the special challenge with film is that the images are constantly moving, so an analytical spectator must develop the habit of looking for key moments, patterns, or images within the film—even during a second or third viewing.

As you watch more films and grow more aware of differences and similarities, the right questions come more readily. At first, though, two guidelines may help initiate this dialogue with a movie:

- Note which elements of the movie strike you as unfamiliar or perplexing.
- Note which elements are repeated to emphasize a point or a perception.

Every movie uses patterns of repetition that are contrasted with strik-ing singular moments. Recognizing these patterns and deciphering why they are important is a first step toward analyzing the meaning of a movie. Why, for instance, do so many scenes in *Rebel without a Cause* (1955) take place in the family homes of the characters? Why, in George Cukor's *The Women* (1939), is black and white used for all the scenes except the fashion show? Even if you do not determine the answers to these ques-tions while you are watching the movie, asking them is the key to a good analysis. These questions can be as elementary as the following:

- What does the title mean in relation to the story?
- Why does the movie start the way it does?
- When was the film made?
- Why are the opening credits presented in such a manner against this particular background?
- Why does the film conclude on this image?
- How is this movie similar to or different from the Hollywood movies I have seen recently or from those of an older generation?
- Does this film resemble any foreign films I know of?
- Is there a pattern of striking camera movements, perhaps long shots or dissolves or abrupt transitions (see pp. 60–64)?
- Which three or four sequences are the most important?

When Andrew Sarris, a critic for the *Village Voice*, saw Martin Scorsese's *After Hours* (1985), he found the opening sequence not only bizarre, but partly inexplicable; to some extent, his review evolved from that experience. On seeing Howard Hawks's *His Girl Friday* (1940) for the first time, most contemporary audiences would probably remark, and perhaps have difficulty with, the rapidity of the dialogue, and following up this simple observation with more careful thinking could bring some of the brilliance of this movie into focus. The 2006 *Stranger than Fiction* is about the humdrum life of IRS agent Harold Crick (Will Ferrell), but quickly the story takes an unexpected turn when he begins to hear a voice in his head that seems to be narrating his life. When he identifies the voice as that of a famous novelist, Karen Eiffel (Emma Thompson), who has made him a character in her story, the partly seri-ous, partly comic drama becomes about his attempt to convince Eiffel not to conclude her story, as she intends, with his death. Needless to say, a movie like this unsettles viewers' expectations and provokes numer-ous questions. Is the film simply slapstick comedy based in fantasy, or does it suggest more serious questions about how we live our lives and make decisions? What does it mean that the humor suddenly grows dark when an impending and perhaps inevitable death threatens the comedy of the main character? How does this bizarre mystery about his narrated life relate to Harold's new romance with the woman he is auditing? Might the film even be commenting on the formulas of narrative and storytelling and their relation to the lives we live? Sooner or later, viewers must deal with these implicit questions if they are to make sense of the film. The number and nature of your questions—both about what you see and about how it is shown—could vary infinitely depending on the movie or movies being discussed. Potentially, any and every aspect of the film is important. Talking about *You Only Live Once* (1937), Fritz Lang noted, for instance, a seemingly minor detail that, if the studio had allowed it to remain, would have focused on a central theme in the film: "I wanted to have a kind of ironic touch when Fonda and Sidney flee from the law and she goes and buys him some cigarettes, which ultimately provide the means of his betrayal. I wanted her to buy Lucky Strike cigarettes to stress the irony of the bad luck they bring him." Learn to jot down information about props, costumes, camera positions, and so on, even during a first screening, and then choose the most telling evidence. These are the first steps in developing a strong and perceptive argument. Note how one student used his questions about two striking features of *The Women* to focus a short analysis of that film:

Roger Malone

By most counts, *The Women* seems to be a standard movie about social relations in a 1930s society. There are, though, two odd twists to the movie that should catch anybody's eye: First, there is not a single man in the movie and, second, in the middle of this black-and-white film, there is a rather long fashion show sequence in full color. Why these twists, and are they something more than gimmicks?

The women at the heart of this movie are in some ways independent and resourceful. Their lives are not, though, "liberated" in any modern sense, for men are constantly being discussed and influencing the behavior of all the women. The physical absence of all the men from the screen consequently becomes an ironic way of suggesting how powerfully present those men are in the lives of women. For the women in this movie, even when men are not there, they are there.

The fashion show sequence seems related to this same idea. The sets, the costumes, and the actresses in *The Women* are all stunning, and the female characters all seem concerned with how they and their surroundings appear—especially to men. What could be a more accurate and appropriate centerpiece for the movie than a fashion show of women showing other women how to appear and what to wear? What could be a more effective way to underline the importance of this moment in the film than by making it the only color sequence in the movie?

The Women was made in 1939 by the same studio that produced *The Wizard of Oz* the same year. In *The Women,* however, the flight into color does not last as long as Dorothy's, and for these women, the yellow brick road is fashion itself. Through its unusual twists, moreover, it seems to make an often-recognized point: Even when you cannot see behind the curtain, at the center of the action, hiding there is still a man.

TAKING NOTES

Good film essays require more than one viewing, either of the film itself or of the usually more available video version (see pp. 132–134). With one viewing, it is nearly impossible to see all the subtleties and complexities in a movie and, at the same time, to take notes on this information. Ideally, in fact, a first viewing can be a more or less note-free viewing during which you enjoy the film on its most immediate level. With the second screening (and ideally a third), you can begin to take more careful and detailed notes. One viewing of a film you intend to discuss intelligently is never sufficient.

Often, though, that needed second or third screening may not be possible, especially if the film is older, foreign, or not in wide distribution. In such cases, despite the difficulty in taking your eyes off the screen momentarily, it is important to take notes of some sort during a first-and-only viewing. If more than one screening is possible, notes can be increasingly detailed and complete.

Preliminary notes can be simply a shorthand version of the questions and dialogue a movie generates in your mind. No one can— or wants to—note everything that appears, especially because taking notes takes your eyes away from other information on the screen. The trick is to learn to make economical use of your time and to recognize key sequences, shots, or narrative facts. (One useful exercise is to limit yourself to noting, with as much detail as possible, what you consider the three or four most important scenes, shots, or sequences in a film.) Depending on our interests, we all respond to different points or figures in a movie (at least on one level), but most films offer recognizable dramatic moments or major themes that signal an audience to attend to what is happening: the opening sequence in *Citizen Kane* (1941), when "Rosebud" is first pronounced; the climactic death of the father in Douglas Sirk's *Written on the Wind* (1957); the use of sound in Lang's *M* (1931); the dramatic impact of isolated scenes between Bogart and Bacall in practically any of their movies; or the explosive moment when Mookie breaks the window of the pizza parlor in Spike Lee's *Do the Right Thing* (1989). Even when a film denies or parodies these dramatic moments or themes—as in Chantal Akerman's renowned *Jeanne Dielman* (1975) and the films of Iranian director Abbas Kiarostami, such as *Taste of Cherry* (1997)—those variations from the norm may be the central point that a viewer should note and attempt to make sense of.

In noting this kind of information, be as specific and concrete as possible; record not only the figures and objects in the frame (the content), but also how the frame itself and its photographic qualities (the form) are used to define that content through camera angles, lighting, the use of depth and surface, and editing techniques. A person preparing to write about *Meet Me in St. Louis* (1944) might note the father's role in this family of women or the odd, macabre scenes with the youngest daughter, Tootie. With practice, however, that writer would also be able to jot down information about the theatrical use of space in specific scenes or the spectacular use of bright color. Similarly, even a student new to R. W. Fassbinder's films would probably catch some of the major motifs or salient moments in *The Marriage of Maria Braun* (1979): the numerous ironic turns in sexual relations that seem so bound up with financial matters or the confusion about whether, at the conclusion, the heroine does or does not commit suicide. A bit more advanced viewer, however, might also remark on the careful overlapping and disjunctions between the sound track and the images: Perhaps the student will describe the subtle but powerful scene in which Oswald casually plays a concerto measure on a piano that alternates with the same phrase in the sound track's background music, or perhaps he or she will note how, during that melodramatic closing sequence, the radio in the background blares a World Cup championship match.

Most writers develop a shorthand system for technical information: *pov* for "point of view shot" or *ls* for "long shot" (a shot that shows, for example, the whole of a figure from a distance, as opposed to a close-up of a face or a hand). Some of these are standardized abbreviations that are easy to learn and use when taking notes (the abbreviations do not, of course, appear in this form in your final essay):

cu	close-up (showing only the character's head, for example)
xcu	extreme close-up (perhaps showing a detail of that head, such as the eyes)
ms	medium shot (somewhere between a close-up and a full shot, showing most but not all of a figure)
fs	full or long shot (revealing the character's entire body in the frame)
3/4s	three-quarter shot (showing only about three-quarters of the characters' bodies)
ps	pan shot (the point of view pivots from left to right or vice versa but without changing its vertical axis)
s/rs	shot/reverse shot pattern (the point of view shows, for example, a person looking at someone and then shows the individual being looked at)
ct	cut (when the film changes from one image to another)
lt	long take (the film does not cut to another image for an unusually long time)
crs	crane shot (the point of view films an outdoor scene from high above)
trs	tracking shot (the entire point of view moves, on tracks or on a dolly, following, for instance, a walking figure). You can indicate the direction that the camera tracks by using arrows:

$$\uparrow \qquad \longrightarrow \qquad \curvearrowright$$

la	low angle (the point of view is low, tilted upward)
ha	high angle (the point of view is above, tilted downward); the exact angle can be made clearer by using arrows)

Ultimately, each individual develops a personal shorthand and other abbreviations to record accurately the details of a scene or sequence. (These and other terms are more fully defined in Chapter 3.) Often, for annotations on sound or dialogue, a key phrase or word may be what allows you to give a more precise description of the scene or sequence later. Sometimes, these annotations may even take the form of a quick sketch, as with this student's attempt to note how, with these five shots (Figures 2.02– 2.06) from the "Odessa Steps" sequence in *The Battleship Potemkin* (1925), Eisenstein's editing of the soldiers' attack on a mother and child works to create conflicts in the movement within each shot.

No one will exhaustively annotate an entire film. Anticipating a specific argument and essay, everyone will focus on different kinds of information, from themes and characters to technical elements and editing structures. If a writer wishes to analyze the famous shower sequence in Alfred Hitchcock's *Psycho* (1960), for instance, some preliminary notes might look something like this: "(1) ms Marion and Norman, cramped space, 'trapped,' birds, eyes, sexual tension; (2) classical painting/peephole; (3) 90° cu then pov N at undressing M; (4) shower, tight space; (5) murder: quick cuts, cu's knife, face, flesh, M's pov; (6) M clawing curtain, cu drain, cu eye." This is a quick sketch that needs to be filled in later. If a second viewing is possible, more dialogue or details can be added. Yet, beginning with these notes, a writer could develop a fairly sophisticated and rigorous reading of this key scene.

Figure 2.02 cu—sold legs.

Figure 2.03 fs—moth. & ch/sol.

VISUAL MEMORY AND REFLECTION

Preliminary notes and sketches will form the basis for a good argument, however, only if the writer elaborates on them shortly after seeing the movie by filling in the shorthand with more carefully measured descriptions. Jean Mitry, a renowned French film historian, once said his most important asset was an unusually precise visual memory. The best writers about film either come equipped with or are able to develop a sharp auditory and visual memory, which allows them to remember details about a movie. (Remember: A memory can be trained and developed; no one should seek to justify careless viewing and annotation by claiming a "bad memory.") The sooner one can go back to those preliminary notes, the better, for then the memory can be triggered to add more specifics and place images in the context of the larger story and other narrative issues. Returning to his notes on *Psycho,* that writer might recall other images that emphasize eyes in the movie and make connections between the hole in the wall and the close-up of the shower drain or between the cramped space of Norman's den and that of the shower. He or she might realize that

Figure 2.04 fs—sol/moth. & ch.

the sequence is remarkably balanced and frighteningly logical in being extended as it is until the final close-ups of the dark drain and the dead Marion's open eye. On further reflection, that writer might decide that, based on the opening shots of the film, *Psycho* is about "looking" and the sexual or gendered implications of looking.

When you've reviewed your notes, the shape and direction of your argument may begin to appear in an idea of what you wish to say about this movie. Whether or not you are prepared before a first viewing, possible arguments and topics should begin to present themselves as you begin to add to and develop those preliminary notes. While going over notes on *The Marriage of Maria Braun,* one student discovered that her initial perception of the movie as a glossy melodrama was complicated by those strange technical maneuvers with the sound track that she had recorded in her notes; her essay then discussed the ways in which the sound track signaled the splits and divisions between the main character's private, emotional life and her public, social life (Figure 2.07). Using the shorthand notes on Eisenstein's *The Battleship Potemkin* shown earlier, that student started a shot-by-shot analysis that moved from those notes to a clear verbal description of those images. Note how a precise description of this sort can function alone as the foundation for critical analysis:

Figure 2.05 ms—moth. & ch.

In Eisenstein's *The Battleship Potemkin* (1925), the "Odessa
Steps" sequence combines powerful human images with graphic
visual patterns. I will highlight five shots at the center of this
sequence to illustrate its formal construction and emotional direction. First, early in the sequence, there is a shot of the soldiers' legs
marching methodically, on a diagonal line, downward from left to
right. Not long after that image comes a shot of a mother walking up the middle of the image with her wounded child, toward
the soldiers, on a line which directly confronts the direction of
the soldiers' movement as they march down on her from above.
The angle of the shot changes again, and now, from behind and
to the right of the soldiers, we see them fire their rifles directly
toward the woman and child (here the camera's off-center perspective intersects with the line that connects the aim of the rifles and
the movement of the woman toward them, making the spectator a

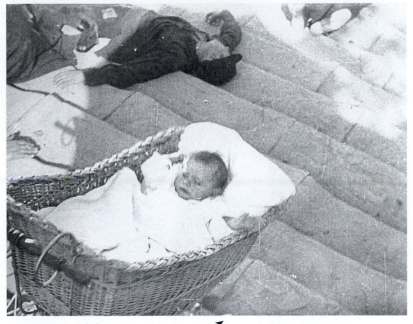

Figure 2.06 ms—baby.

kind of visual mediator). That image then changes to a shot of the same woman as she is about to be killed, seen now much closer and looking up toward the camera (which is the direction of the soldiers). Shortly afterward, a baby in a carriage tumbles down the steps, another child-victim propelled to its death by the downward force of the soldiers' diagonal. That the direction of this child's fall is now from the lower left to the upper right of the frame may suggest, though, the "uprising" that is soon to follow these images. Beyond the obvious sacrifice of the weak and innocent, these five shots place the viewer at the graphic intersection where the lines of an implacable mechanical force collide with the lines of human resistance.

Finally, the writer on *Psycho* begins to focus an essay on looking and sexuality with the central shower sequence: *Psycho* becomes a film about the violence implicit in the sexual and gendered dynamics of men and women looking at each other, and Marion's murder becomes the most

Figure 2.07 *The Marriage of Maria Braun:* A melodrama made cramped and uncomfortable by the camera framing.

dramatic example of people trapped in the violence and horror of their sexuality. Or, as Donald Spoto refined his notes,

> The psychological shock of the sequence, however, derives from the fact that the character with whom we have identified has been brutally elimi-nated. We have felt her frustration, hoped she would escape the police, enjoyed her innocent teasing of Norman, shared her sense of release at the decision to make amends and experienced the first moments of that cleansing shower. And, through Hitchcock's brilliant direction, we have felt her hideous pain, and her inability to avoid the persistent stabs as she turns around in the shower. The cleansing water turns to blood. We have followed every step of the way in her descent from the banal to the horrific. Now, seeing her last sight through her eyes, we watch her left hand slowly sliding down the tiles in a last attempt to "scratch and claw," as Norman has put it, out of this shower-turned-coffin. She slowly turns and, leaning against the wall with her last breaths, slides down into death. She stares, with gradually closing lids, then reaches out—for us. But we pull back, so she grabs the shower curtain for final support, rip-ping it from the hooks as she falls forward and over the edge of the tub. One more glance at the cleansing laver, from a point under the shower nozzle, and then in one of the most brilliant images in any film—we follow the bloodied water spiralling down the drain. In an extraordinary

lap dissolve, we emerge from the darkness of the drain out from behind her eye, open and stilled in death. The journey into the depths of the "normal" psyche has ended in tragedy. The veneer of normality has been shattered at her (and our) peril. And the close-up of the eye links us by association with Norman's eye during the peeping scene earlier, and with our own role throughout as peeping Toms. All the characters of this film are indeed one character, and through the use of alternating subjective camera technique, that character is the individual viewer. (372–74)

Few of us are inclined to work back through notes immediately after seeing a movie. Yet a prompt review of one's notes is extremely useful and could make the difference between a dull and hazy response to a film and a compelling and subtle one. Methodical notes allow a viewer to map accurately what happens in a movie, to record details about the subject and its meaning that would otherwise soon fade from memory. Unless one has continual access to the film or a script, it is difficult to retain these facts, and without them, anything you have to say will probably appear much too impressionistic. When you go over the film and the key sequences in your notes, ideas begin to take shape. When you can support those ideas with concrete descriptions from the movie, an argument becomes dramatically more convincing.

Exercises

1. Before seeing a film, read two or three reviews or commentaries about it. Then, based on those reviews, jot down three expectations about the film. What will probably be the most important features of the film? Specific characters? The sound? Do these expectations lead you to look for certain themes or types of stories?

2. Choose a single short sequence from a film and annotate it as precisely as you can. Describe those annotations in clear, precise prose. Are there any conclusions you can draw or interpretations you would make about the sequence?

3

FILM TERMS AND TOPICS FOR FILM ANALYSIS AND WRITING

Developing a sense of how to question movie images and take notes on them goes hand in hand with an ability to direct those questions toward specific topics for analysis. Questions and notes should lead to more questions and partial or full answers. This path leads to an essay focused on particular themes and techniques in a movie. A major part of this process is developing a vocabulary with which to ask those questions properly, to describe what you see and think, and to help you focus and organize your analysis. Being able to notice and then comment on a significant "shot/reverse shot" editing pattern in *Milk* (2008) or to describe the "predominance of close-ups" in *The Tourist* (2010) is not only good for classroom conversation, but also allows a good writer to make finer, more accurate discriminations and evaluations and to situate a film within the larger tradition of film history and analysis. These kinds of discriminations should begin to point you toward a topic for a paper.

Every discipline has its own special language or use of words that allows it to discuss its subject with precision and subtlety. A literary critic, for example, needs to distinguish between a metaphor and a simile, because these terms describe different rhetorical figures that, in turn, refer to different sorts of perceptions. "My love is like a red, red rose" (simile) is different from "My love is the red rose of life" (metaphor), and the person who can appreciate that difference will read and interpret those lines better. Similarly, a knowledgeable basketball fan will be able to summarize quickly and evaluate the action of a game if he or she knows a specialized vocabulary that includes terms such as *jump shot, pick,* and *fast break.*

With film, too, a critical vocabulary allows you to view a movie more accurately and formulate your perceptions more easily. Consider the term *frame.* In writing about film, *frame* refers to the rectangle that contains the image: the frame of the movie screen itself, which does not change during a movie, and, more important, the camera frame, which regularly changes its relationship to the objects being filmed. Being aware of this term and its uses means you will be more sensitive to how the camera frame controls what you see and how you see it. You will be able to note, for instance, that the camera frame may include certain actions and exclude others and that the angle at which it is placed or its distance from a person adds considerably to what the filmmaker is trying to say. As one student observed of a recent movie, "Although the scene seems to be a typical family gathering, the viewer becomes aware that something is wrong or unsettled because the camera frame is slightly tilted and unusually crowded with characters and furniture." What may sometimes go unnoticed is brought to light through the accurate use of a term.

THEMES

Going over your notes, your first step may be trying to identify the major themes of the movie, which often comes down to stepping back and asking what this film is "about": the triumph of good over evil in *Harry Potter and the Deathly Hallows* (2010), for example, or reluctant heroism before unimaginable brutality in *Schindler's List* (1993).These themes, in many cases, become the foundation for an analysis because they point to the main ideas in a movie. They are not, strictly speaking, the "moral" or message of the movie; they are the large and the small ideas that help to explain the actions and events in it. Ask, for example, the following:

- Who are the central characters?
- What do they represent in themselves and in relation to each other? The importance of individuality, or society? Human strength, or human compassion?
- How do their actions create a story with a meaning or constellation of meanings?
- Does the story emphasize the benefits of change, or endurance?
- What kind of life or what actions does the film wish you to value or criticize, and why?
- If there is not a coherent message or story, why not?
- How does the movie make you feel at the end? Happy? Depressed? Confused? Why?

Having sketched some major and minor themes in a film, the writer needs to refine these in terms of the specific situation and aims of the movie. The more sensitive a writer's vocabulary, the more refined his or her perception and argument will be. Thus *alienation* may very well describe the broadest thematic lines of Charlie Chaplin's *City Lights* (1931), Frank Capra's *You Can't Take It with You* (1938), Bernardo Bertolucci's *The Conformist* (1970), and Martin Scorsese's *Shutter Island* (2010).

This may be a good start, but a sharp analysis demands that the writer make finer distinctions about the historical, stylistic, and structural presentations of that theme in each movie. Does the alienation seem inevitable or, perhaps, even desirable? Does it lead to new knowledge, or is it a disaster that could have been avoided? Is it presented as a tragic or a comic problem in the movie? Writing about *The Conformist*, a student might refine the theme of alienation by observing that here it relates to the protagonist's sexuality and the fascist period in Italy and that, unlike the first two movies (and, to some extent, the fourth), the movie never really resolves this alienation. He or she might further specify and clarify that argument by describing how the main character regularly seems entrapped and isolated by the rigorous framing of the camera (Figure 3.01) and by the many frames within the image as a whole (door frames, window frames, and so on). Note, however, that this kind of refinement of alienation in *The Conformist* does not attempt to fashion an oversimplified and inapplicable moral. One cannot say, "In *The Conformist*, alienation is an evil which dooms the character to misery."

While identifying themes provides an important foundation for your analysis, writing about the movies involves a wide range of special terms

Figure 3.01 The frames within the framing of *The Conformist* (1970).

that will help you to organize and clarify your topic. The remainder of this chapter discusses the most important of these terms as they are used to discuss four dimensions of the movies:

1. The connections between the movies and other artistic traditions, such as literature and painting
2. The theatrical dimension of the film image, or of its mise-en-scène
3. The compositions of the movie, achieved through camera positions and editing
4. The use of sound in the film

Depending on your topic, any or all of these dimensions and their vocabulary may be central to your essay.

FILM AND THE OTHER ARTS

Although the movies are one of the youngest of the arts, they have absorbed the structures and forms of many older arts. Not surprisingly, therefore, writing about film requires some of the critical language of these other literary and visual arts: We speak of *plot* and *character* in both films and novels, and terms such as *point of view* are part of the critical vocabulary of painting, literature, and the movies. Borrowed terminology allows a critic to make important connections with other fields; it also demands that a writer be sensitive to how terms and structures change when they are applied to film. Here we will look at three related terms that film studies share with the literary and visual arts: *narrative, characters,* and *point of view.*

Narrative

When most of us refer to the movies, we are referring to narrative movies alone, not documentaries or experimental films. A *narrative* can be divided into different components:

- The *story* is all the events that are presented to us or that we can infer have happened.
- The *plot* is the arrangement or construction of those events in a certain order or structure.
- *Narration* refers to the perspective that organizes the plot according to a certain emotional, physical, or intellectual point of view.

Thus all films that sketch the life of Napoleon would tell the same story: his birth, his rise to power, the French Revolution, its aftermath, and his exile to Elba. The plots in these different movies may, however, be structured and arranged in various ways: One could begin with Napoleon's last days at Elba and tell his story through a series of flashbacks (showing events that occurred earlier than the ones just shown); another could start with his birth and move chronologically through his life. Finally, the narration of these actions may vary considerably: one film could use an *omniscient narration,* which presents the elements of the plot from potentially any possible angle, while another uses a *restricted narration* that limits what is shown and known to one or two characters.

Always ask yourself how the narrative of the film you are watching is constructed. Is it, first of all, a movie with a story line? If not, why not? Is the story told chronologically, or does the plot rearrange events in an unusual temporal order? Is there a reason for that particular plot structure? What in the story is left out in the actual plot construction? Are there reasons for including some material and omitting other material? Does the way the story is told become a prominent feature of the film and thus a central factor in an analysis of it? How is the narration made apparent? Is there a *voice-over,* in which a character's voice is heard describing events and thus makes it clear that he or she is organizing the plot? Are there technical elements that give dramatic indications about the presence of a narrative perspective, such as the change from black and white to color in *The Wizard of Oz* (1939) or Mike Figgis's use of four different quadrants depicting four simultaneous actions on a single screen in his *Timecode* (2000)? Is the movie especially concerned with questions of time and history, which may, in turn, influence how the plot is constructed through, for instance, *flashbacks* or, more rarely, *flashforwards*? What propels the story? A mystery, as in *The Big Sleep* (1946)? A desire to reach a goal, as in *Legally Blonde* (2001)? Or, is it difficult to say, as in some modern movies in which the plot seems to have no definite direction?

The various relationships among a story, its plot, and a narrative style are numerous. When most of us think of a narrative film, however, we probably have in mind what is often called a *classical narrative* (Figure 3.02). To discuss any kind of film narrative, it is useful to have some sense of this important narrative form. Usually, a classical narrative has the following:

- A plot development in which there is a logical relation between one event and another
- A sense of closure at the end (a happy or a tragic ending, for example)
- Stories that are focused on characters
- A narration that attempts to be more or less objective or realistic

Figure 3.02 The narrative of *Casablanca* (1942) employs many of the features of classical narrative: a plot propelled by a central character (Bogart as Rick), a realistic depiction of events, and a dramatic sense of closure (as Ilsa and Rick sacrifice their love for a greater patriotic good).

Not all classical narratives are the same, of course, and many fine essays are about the variations and innovations within this model. One student, for example, began his paper on Howard Hawks's *The Big Sleep* by observing the following:

Bill Evans

This classic mystery story does not make complete sense. It seems as if the complicated plot has lost track of the story, and frequently it is very difficult to follow the logic of who killed whom and why. Nonetheless, *The Big Sleep* remains a model of classical filmmaking in the way it concentrates all the action on the main characters, Bogart and Bacall. If the plot is confused, these characters make you forget that confusion and realize that the story is about them.

In the following paragraphs, Gerald Mast looks at the narrative structure as it applies to many Hawks films (such as *To Have and Have Not* [1944] and *His Girl Friday* [1940]). Note how Mast first places his analysis in the literary tradition of narrative and then moves to a discussion of plots constructed around the notion of "surprising inevitability."

What is a good story? First, there is the construction of an action—not just enumerating a string of events but organizing those events into a coherent and powerful shape. The construction of a narrative action relies on a very interesting paradox, of which Hawks was well aware. On the one hand, the events in a narrative must seem to flow spontaneously, naturally, surprisingly; nothing must be expected, nothing foreseen. On the other hand, the events in a narrative must be prepared for, motivated, foreshadowed; nothing is unexpected, everything foreseen. On the one hand, everything that happens to King Lear is a surprise. On the other, everything in the play proceeds from Kent's command in the beginning to "See better, Lear." It is surprising that Emma Woodhouse discovers that it is Mr. Knightley whom she really must marry; yet everything in *Emma* points the way to this inevitable and inescapable discovery. The paradox of narrative construction is that it synthesizes the accidents of nature—which seem random—and the patterns of logic—which are fixed; the outcome of events is simultaneously inevitable yet surprising to the reader or viewer when the inevitable occurs. The narrative that is insufficiently spontaneous and surprising is familiarly condemned as contrived, overplotted, unnatural, and stilted; the narrative that is insufficiently patterned is familiarly condemned as random, wandering, arbitrary, and formless.

How does Hawks' story construction relate to this paradox of surprising inevitability? In over forty years of filmmaking, collaborating with over a dozen major writers, Howard Hawks builds every story in an identical four-part structure. The first part is a prologue that either (1) establishes the conflict in a past or present close relationship of the major characters (this is the usual pattern of Ben Hecht's scripts for Hawks) or (2) initiates a conflict by the collision of two apparently opposite characters upon their initial meeting (this is the usual Furthman–Faulkner pattern). The second and third parts develop the central conflict established in the first, either by letting one of the conflicting characters or life styles dominate in the second part, then the other in the third, or by letting one of the characters work alone in the second part, then both of them together in the third. And the fourth section resolves the central conflict, often by a return to the original physical

setting of the prologue, but in which setting the warring characters now
see themselves and one another in a new light. Occasionally Hawks adds
a very brief epilogue or "tag" to return the narrative full circle to its
beginning. Whatever else one can say about this narrative structure,
it gives a Hawks story the firmness of shape, the elegance, economy,
and symmetry that allow surprising events to transpire within the firm
logic and structure of a controlled pattern. (30–31)

Not all movies are classical narratives or even narratives. A large
number of independent and foreign films create narratives—sometimes
referred to as *alternative narratives* or *postclassical narratives*—that
are outside the classical tradition or that may intentionally confront that
tradition to tell their stories distinctively, such as Wong Kar-wai's 1997
Happy Together and its wandering tale of two young men who leave
Hong Kong to drift through the backstreets of Buenos Aires. When you
watch a movie that seems to avoid a traditional story line or to tell its story
in an unusual or, perhaps, confusing way, ask yourself how the movie is
organizing its plot and narration and what it is trying to achieve. Do the
characters seem unformed or undirected in a way that's important to
the meaning of the film? Why might the narrative lack a forward linear
progress? Does the narrative seem to be telling two or more stories that
are difficult to connect, as in *Hiroshima Mon Amour* (1959), in which
the story of a woman and her Nazi lover is told alongside the story of the
bombing of Hiroshima? Does the movie have a confusing beginning or an
unresolved conclusion? Why? How do these or other narrative strategies
relate to the stories being told? About *Hiroshima Mon Amour,* a writer
might, after some thought, begin by observing that both stories concern
World War II and are told by two newly met lovers; the difficulty in the
narrative structure might then be related to the woman's pain in organizing and communicating her memories to someone from a completely different culture but with a similar historical crisis. Once you have learned
to recognize classical narrative forms, you should be more aware of the
variety of ways in which stories can be told.

Many other films are nonnarrative: They do not tell stories, or they
subsume stories within organizational structures other than narrative.
For instance, there are experimental films that avoid stories and instead
investigate questions or aesthetic concerns unrelated to narrative, such
as the abstract patterns of light and shadow on film. Avant-garde filmmaker Maya Deren's *Meshes of the Afternoon* (1943), for example,
repeats images of a shrouded woman walking and unexplained images
of a key and a knife to create a film that seems more like a dream than
a story. A different kind of nonnarrative film, documentary cinema may

Figure 3.03 *Waltz with Bashir* (2008) is an experimental documentary that overlays real people and events with animation. The result is part diary, part essay, part newsreel, and part surreal memory.

present real events, such as a typical day at a factory or a religious ritual of a Native American tribe, without organizing those events as a story. Israeli filmmaker Ari Folman's *Waltz with Bahsir* (2008) is a personal documentary describing Folman's experience of the Lebanon invasion in 1982: his interviews with former friends and soldiers struggle to determine what really happened during those traumatic events, and he stretches the boundaries of traditional documentary by recreating real people and places as animated figures and images (Figure 3.03). When viewing experimental or documentary cinema, begin with some basic questions:

- If the film does not seem organized as a story, what seems to be the model for its organization: A dream? An argument? A news report? Or some other form? How does that model suggest a way to understand the film?
- What are the formal features or organizations that stand out? A series of contrasts? Repetitions? Disconnected fragments? Or some other pattern? Why is that pattern important to the meaning of the film?

Characters

Characters are another common topic for analysis in literature, drama, and film. They are the individuals who populate narrative and nonnarrative films. Whether they are the main characters or minor characters, they normally focus the action and, often, the themes of a movie (Figure 3.04). Often, a discussion of film concentrates exclusively on what happens to the characters or how they change. *My Dinner with André* (1981), which films the dinner conversation between two men, could more accurately be described as being about two characters telling stories than as being a story about two characters. Both mainstream movies, like *Public Enemies* (2009), and more experimental films, like *Crumb* (1994), focus their narratives almost exclusively on the biography of their main character, the rise and fall of the infamous bank robber John Dillinger (in the first case) and underground cartoonist Robert Crumb (in the second). Keep in mind that an analysis of characters in a movie can be boring or seem simpleminded if you approach them as if they are merely reflections of real people or if you blur the difference between the real historical person, the actor playing the role, and the character. Yet if you remain attuned to the variety in character types and constructions, you can begin to see

Figure 3.04 Stanley Kubrick's *Full Metal Jacket* (1987) presents characters in a more extreme and disturbing way than in many films. It follows the development of young men who, drafted to become soldiers during the Vietnam War, are transformed into killing machines.

subtleties and complications in how characters function and what they mean in different films. As an exercise, choose three different characters—those portrayed by Lillian Gish in *Broken Blossoms* (1919), Lauren Bacall in *The Big Sleep*, and Tilda Swinton in *I Am Love* (2009), for example—and try to describe how and why those characters are so different.

You can begin an analysis of characters by asking yourself if those characters seem or are meant to seem realistic. What makes them realistic? Are they defined by their clothes, their conversation, or something else? If they are not realistic, why not, and why are they meant to seem strange or fantastic? Do the characters seem to fit the setting of the story? Does the movie focus mainly on one or two characters, as in *The Big Sleep*, or on many, as in *Gosford Park* (2001), in which there doesn't seem to be a central character? Do the characters change and, if so, in what ways? What values do the characters seem to represent? What do they say about such matters as independence, sexuality, and political belief?

Normally, we take characters for granted, and these are a sampling of the kinds of questions you can begin to direct at characters to make more sense of them and determine why they are important.

Point of View

Like narrative, *point of view* is a term that film shares with the literary and visual arts. In the broadest sense, it refers to the position from which something is seen and, by implication, the way that point of view determines what you see. In the simplest sense, the point of view is purely physical. My point of view regarding a house across the street will, for example, be very different if I am looking from the rooftop of my house or from the basement window. In a more sophisticated sense, point of view can be psychological or cultural. For example, a child's point of view about a dentist's office will probably not be the same as an adult's.

In the same way, we can talk about the point of view that the camera has in relationship to a person or action or even the point of view that a narrative directs at its subject (Figure 3.05). Usually, movies use an objective point of view so that most of what is shown is not confined to any one person's perspective. In *Gone with the Wind* (1939) or *Gandhi* (1982), the audience sees scenes and events (the Battle of Atlanta, epic encounters in India) that are supposedly objective in their scope and accuracy, beyond the knowledge or perspective of any one person. In specific scenes, however, that audience may be aware that they are seeing another character only through Rhett or Gandhi's eyes, and in these cases, the camera is recreating that individual's more subjective point of view. Some movies experiment with the possibilities of point

Figure 3.05 Alfred Hitchcock's *Rear Window* (1945) is a film explicitly organized around the point of view of a photographer confined to a wheelchair. As he and his girlfriend watch the secret lives of his New York neighbors, he discovers both the power and the dangers of a point of view.

of view: In *Apocalypse Now* (1979), we seem to see the whole story from Captain Willard's (Martin Sheen's) point of view; he introduces the story as something that has already happened to him, but despite this indication of historical objectivity, many of the scenes recreate his personal, nightmarish perspective on the war in Vietnam.

Point of view is a central term in writing about films, because films are basically about seeing the world in a certain way. Pay attention to point of view by using these two general guidelines:

1. Observe how and when the camera creates the point of view of a character.
2. Notice if the story is told mostly from an objective point of view or from the subjective perspective of one person.

Ask yourself in what ways the point of view is determining what you see. Does it limit or control your vision in any way? What can you tell about the characters whose eyes you see through? Are they aggressive? Suspicious? Clever? In love?

Comparative Essays and Adaptations

Because the movies incorporate the traditions of books, plays, and even sculpture and painting, terms such as *narrative, character,* and *point of view* are not only useful, but necessary in analyzing film. Often, these terms provide the basis for a comparative essay that examines a book and its adaptation as a film or, especially in recent years, the adaptation of video games as in films such as *Tron: Legacy* (2010), *Doom* (2005), and *Resident Evil* (2002). Other kinds of comparative essays may compare different versions of the same movie or a group of films by the same director.

When you write a comparative essay of this kind, be sensitive to and careful not only about how these terms connect different art forms, but also about how they highlight differences. Be aware of how the film medium may change the message or meaning of the original book, play, or game. Look, for instance, at how a literary or artistic trope is translated successfully into a movie, as well as at what may be lost; consider how a film adapted from a video game alters or makes use of the way a viewer interacts with the images and sounds. Finally, take into consideration how other social and historical factors may play an important role in the comparison and contrast of different works. The popular Indian adaptation of Jane Austen's novel *Pride and Prejudice* (1813) as *Bride and Prejudice* (2004), for instance, features extraordinary textual changes (including the addition of musical numbers), and a smart comparative analysis would clearly need to examine the South Asian cultural and historical context that influences that adaptation. Less obviously perhaps would be a comparison of Jane Campion's adaptation (1996) of Henry James's *The Portrait of a Lady* (1881), where the gender difference of the female filmmaker and the male author may very well be as important as their historical distance in comparing and understanding the two works.

Whatever line of argument a comparative essay takes, detailed formal evidence is critical. To compare *Apocalypse Now* and Joseph Conrad's novel *Heart of Darkness* (1898), a writer may thus choose to begin with a comparison of the subjective point of view that describes the journey of one Marlow—Captain Willard's—through Vietnam and the journey of the other Marlow into Africa. That comparison will be much sharper and more revealing, however, if the writer can show how certain literary techniques (long sentences full of repetitions, for example) create one point of view and how certain film techniques (the use of light and shadow or exaggerated mise-en-scènes, for instance) create the other. These film techniques are the subject of the rest of this chapter.

MISE-EN-SCÈNE AND REALISM

The *mise-en-scène*, a French term roughly translated as "what is put into the scene" (put before the camera), refers to all those properties of a cinematic image that exist independently of camera position, camera movement, and editing (although a viewer will see these different dimensions united in one image). Mise-en-scène includes lighting, costumes, sets, the quality of the acting, and other shapes and characters in the scene. Many writers mistakenly believe that these theatrical features are a somewhat unsophisticated topic for analysis because they appear to be more a part of a dramatic tradition than of a cinematic tradition. Evaluating the performance of an actor may, for some, seem much less important than analyzing the narrative or the camera work. Yet for many other perceptive critics, the tools and terms of mise-en-scène are the keys to some of the most important features of any movie.

Realism

The major reason that we tend to overlook or undervalue mise-en-scène in the movies is the powerful illusion of realism that is at the heart of the film medium. In many movies, we often presume that "what is put into the scene" is simply what is there; it consequently cannot be analyzed as we would analyze the construction of a plot. We accept the Philadelphia setting of Jonathan Demme's 1993 movie *Philadelphia* as merely the background that was chosen for the battle between a prestigious law firm and a young associate discovered to be HIV positive. But comparing the affluent setting of that film with, say, the mise-en-scène of Philadelphia in the 1976 movie *Rocky* (set in the ethnic neighborhoods of South Philadelphia) or in the 1995 movie *Twelve Monkeys* (set in a Philadelphia of urban squalor and decay) should make it clear that the realism of a place is very malleable. The illusion of realism, in short, is a kind of mise-en-scène that makes us believe that the images are of an everyday world that is simply "there"— one we know and are familiar with. Or, as the Italian neorealist screenwriter Cesare Zavattini argued in 1953, the cinema "must tell reality as if it were a story; there must be no gap between life and what is on the screen" (quoted in Williams 29).

You must learn, however, to be suspicious of realism in the movies, because it can distract you from the many interesting possibilities that mise-en-scène analysis offers. Watching a documentary from another country or an old movie once considered very realistic, you recognize how relative your sense of realism is and how, even when the film-maker may not acknowledge it, the reality of a movie is constructed for a purpose. Simply putting a camera in front of a scene, as one writer has noted, changes the most realistic situation into a kind of theatrical setting. Asked to look more closely at the realism of *Philadelphia*, one student thus corrected her original perception and observed how the mise-en-scène of *Philadelphia* was not just where the central character lived and worked:

> Cecilia A. Graham
>
> The choice of the city of Philadelphia as the setting for the film of the same name clearly evokes connotations which are central to understanding this movie. Since the city itself has historically been referred to as the City of Brotherly Love, *Philadelphia* uses its urban backdrop to set, somewhat ironically, a tale of a gay man whose physical love of a "brother" generates only fear and loathing from the "brothers" in his law firm. At the same time, the mise-en-scène of Philadelphia becomes strangely anonymous in this movie. Most of the action of the movie takes place before the sumptuous modern skyscrapers in a business district which could be any business district and in plush offices whose picture windows show a glittering backdrop of only lights and other buildings. This Philadelphia is, finally, a place without much identity, depth, or individuality, and that seems an appropriate mise-en-scène for a film that largely sanitizes the suffering and confusion of a man battling HIV and an extremely narrow-minded society.

Whether the movie is a documentary or a realistic Hollywood film, a practiced eye might begin an analysis by asking basic questions about the realism of the film and how it is used. Why does the movie try to seem realistic? How does it try to create a realistic scene? What is included, and what is left out? What realistic details in the mise-en-scène relate to the actions of the characters or themes of the movie: the clothing, the homes, the props, or the outdoor world? Treat the mise-en-scène of realistic films with the same analytical sense you might direct at a stage play, in which costumes and sets are never selected casually.

Elements of Mise-en-Scène

In any film, from the most realistic to the most theatrical, there are specific properties of the mise-en-scène at which to direct your attention and from which good paper topics will come.

Settings and *sets* refer to the location or the construction of a location where a scene is filmed. In some movies, you will notice immediately how important the setting and sets are. In *The Cabinet of Dr. Caligari* (1919), for example, the expressionistic set design may be far more interesting to some viewers than the characters or structure of the story: The sets are obviously painted buildings and streets whose distorted angles and shapes are meant to suggest the mental imbalance and social chaos of the characters. One might make the same case for a movie like *Alien* (1979), in which the elaborately twisted passageways of the spaceship and the mysterious construction where the characters discover the alien eggs reverberate with a symbolic significance associated with women and motherhood. Hitchcock uses his settings more ironically, as commentaries on the plot and characters. During the climactic closing of *North by Northwest* (1959), for instance, the hero and the heroine climb across the gigantic faces of the presidents on Mount Rushmore; in a movie so much about U.S. security and government, this use of setting is not only spectacular, but also central to the themes of the movie. The settings in these and other cases are much more than background, and a writer interested in the use of sets and settings like these should start with these questions:

- Do the objects and props in the setting, whether natural ones (like rivers and trees) or artificial ones (like paintings and buildings), have a special significance that relates to the characters or story?
- Does the arrangement of objects, props, and characters within that setting have some significance? (For example, are they crowded together? Do inanimate objects seem to have a life, as they do in a Chaplin movie?)

Although most good films give the setting and its objects nearly as much meaning as the characters, films differ greatly in how they use their settings in relation to characters and stories. Sets and settings may suggest a historical realism, as in *Flags of Our Fathers* (2006) (Figure 3.06); provide images of a character's mind, as in *The Cabinet of Dr. Caligari;* describe the central theme of the film, as does the centrality of the

Figure 3.06 Clint Eastwood's *Flags of Our Father* (2006) is a contemporary film about World War II that relies on a high degree of historical realism to make its mise-en-scène accurate and convincing.

house/home in *Meet Me in St. Louis* (1944); or become as complex and important as the story or characters themselves, as, perhaps, in *The Truman Show* (1998), in which the main character (Jim Carrey) discovers that his life is a television show and that he lives and works on television set (Figure 3.07). In writing about setting, however, one must do more than just describe it: One must seek to discover its significance in relation to the major themes of the film or to other aspects of the film (its system of production or its historical period, for instance). Such a focus will help explain why the setting and the way it is constructed are important.

Use the same rule of thumb in discussing other elements of the mise-en-scène. Whether your interest is acting styles, costumes, or lighting, precise description must be coupled with a sense of why they are important and how they add to the meaning of the movie—that is, how they can become part of a topic for analysis. We all know that an actor is the individual who plays the part of a character in a movie. But *acting style*—how an actor plays a part—differs considerably from film to film and from one decade to the next. When looked at thoughtfully, acting style is a challenging topic to address or a target for focusing an analysis of a specific

Figure 3.07 In *King of Comedy* (1982), Sandra Bernhard's performance as Marsha dramatizes how actors and their styles can make bodies and gestures a dynamic part of a the mise-en-scène.

movie. A writer might, for instance, compare the acting style in an Italian neorealist movie such as *The Bicycle Thieves* (1948), in which some of the actors were people chosen precisely because they had no acting experience, with the mannered style of a British or American actor, like Maggie Smith, whose notion of a realistic performance includes a great deal of studied artifice. The Danish director Carl Dreyer said, "There is no greater experience in a studio than to witness the expression of a sensitive face under the mysterious power of inspiration," and it is precisely that kind of performance that he solicited from Renée Falconetti in the famous close-ups of his *The Passion of Joan of Arc* (1928). In the following paragraph, James Naremore describes, with exemplary sense of details, the remarkable acting style of Sandra Bernhard as Marsha in *The King of Comedy* (1982):

> Bernhard is in fact a club comic, and in many ways she relies on the conventional devices of clowns. She lacks the symmetrical face of "serious" actors like Fonda or Streep, so she pushes her features into grotesque extremes—poking out her lips or curling them up against her long nose, frowning or letting her jaw hang lax. When she moves, she is all angles, a gangling stick figure who looks like an anorexic bobbysoxer; when she speaks, her voice pitches up to the register of a New York teenager on

the verge of hysteria. Nevertheless she inflects her exaggerated behavior in ways quite different from old-fashioned zanies like Fanny Brice
or Martha Raye. Hers is a comedy of neurosis, a mingling of anxiety and
laughter, and she behaves as if the whole weight of an Oedipal scenario
were on her shoulders. (282)

Costumes, as we all know, are the clothes the characters wear. Like
other aspects of the mise-en-scène, they vary along a spectrum from
realistic to extravagant; often, they provide a writer with the key to
a character's identity. James Bond often wears a tuxedo, but Sylvester
Stallone's Rocky prefers to wear as little as possible. In both cases, we
learn something about the character from the costume. Some films, like
Tootsie (1982) and *Hedwig and the Angry Inch* (2001), are largely about
costuming and changing appearances through dress and makeup, and
both films are about how men dress like women to confront or deal with
conventional attitudes about sexual roles. White hats no longer necessarily indicate a good character, but you should continue to question why
characters look and dress the way they do. Do their costumes suggest how
they view themselves, or how they wish to be viewed by others? Does
a character change clothing, as in *Saturday Night Fever* (1977), when
John Travolta becomes a different person by donning his dancing clothes
at night? Do those changes tell you anything about the personality or
the society? Is there a special feature of a costume, such as the baseball
glove that identifies Steve McQueen in *The Great Escape* (1962), that
helps you analyze that character? Again, do not take the costumes of the
mise-en-scène for granted.

Lighting describes the various ways a character or an object or a scene
can be illuminated, either by natural sunlight or from artificial sources
(such as lamps). It allows a filmmaker to direct a viewer's attention in a
certain way or to create a certain atmosphere. We all recognize large distinctions, such as the difference between the bright lighting of an outdoor
scene in a western and the shadowy darkness used in the alleyways of a
gangster film. We probably notice that, in the first case, the lighting creates
a feeling of clarity and optimism, and in the second, a feeling of oppression
and gloom. A more demanding task would be to note and comment on the
more subtle gradations and patterns of lighting that do not dramatically call
attention to themselves. In Bertrand Tavernier's *Sunday in the Country*
(1984), for instance, the softly lit interiors and exteriors seem to recreate
the lighting found in impressionist paintings or, more exactly, the atmos-
pheric lighting found in the 1930s cinema of Jean Renoir, thus resurrect-
ing a vision of the world that the painter grandfather in that movie knows
is fading. In Stanley Kubrick's *Barry Lyndon* (1978), some scenes use

very low light (candlelight, in fact) to emphasize the grotesquely isolated faces of characters who are cut off from one another and from the world that exists in the darkness around them. Whether you notice the lighting immediately or not, be prepared to look for patterns of light and shadows. Are there important graphic patterns (such as sharp shadows), created to highlight a scene or a group of scenes in a movie? Does the lighting or coloring seem totally natural or unusually artificial? Some experimental films make the entire subject of the film the artistic manipulation of light, but any intelligent narrative movie uses lighting with as much a sense of its possibilities and purpose as a painting does (Figure 3.08).

Mise-en-scène, then, is about the theatrics of space as that space is constructed for the camera. This use of space—how it is arranged and how the actors and objects relate within it—can generate exciting topics and commentary on film. The balance or imbalance that relates figures or various planes in the mise-en-scène sometimes says more about that action than does the dialogue: Is, for instance, one character always positioned above another? Is one always in shadows? Likewise, in comparing two sets or settings in a film, you may discover important themes that would otherwise not be noticed: Do catastrophes, for instance, occur only in the city, or only on land? A cinematic mise-en-scène is different from but as complex as a theatrical mise-en-scène, and a writer about

Figure 3.08 In *Close Encounters of the Third Kind* (1977), spectacular lighting techniques and graphics are the heart of the movie.

film should aim for the same acuteness and subtlety demonstrated in the following analysis of the mise-en-scène (specifically the setting) in Buster Keaton's *Our Hospitality* (1923):

> Mise-en-scène functions, not in isolated moments, but in relation to the narrative system of the entire film. *Our Hospitality,* like most of Buster Keaton's films, exemplifies how mise-en-scène can economically advance the narrative and create a pattern of motifs. And since the film is a comedy, we shall find that the mise-en-scène also creates gags. *Our Hospitality,* then, exemplifies what we shall find in our study of every film technique: an individual element will almost always have several functions, not just one.
>
> Consider, for example, how the settings function within the narrative of *Our Hospitality.* They help divide the film into scenes and contrast those scenes. The film begins with a prologue showing how the feud between the McKays and the Canfields results in the deaths of the young Canfield and the husband of the McKay family. We see the McKays living in a shack and are left in suspense about the fate of the baby, Willie. Willie's mother flees with her son from their southern home to the North (action narrated to us mainly by an intertitle). The main action begins years later, with the grown-up Willie living in New York. There are a number of gags concerning early nineteenth-century life in the metropolis, contrasting sharply with the prologue scene. We are led to wonder how this locale will relate to the southern scenes, and soon Willie receives word that he has inherited his parents' home in the South. A series of amusing short scenes follows as he takes a primitive train back to his birthplace. Here Keaton uses real landscapes, but by laying the railroad tracks in different ways, he exploits the landscapes for surprising and unusual comic effects. The rest of the film deals with Willie's movements in the southern town and in the vicinity. On the day of his arrival he wanders around and gets into a number of comic situations. That night he stays in the Canfield house itself, since the law of hospitality has made it the only safe place for him. And, finally, an extended chase occurs the next day, moving through the countryside and back to the Canfield house for the end of the feud. Thus the action depends heavily on shifts of setting that establish Willie's two journeys, as baby and as man, and later his wanderings around to escape his enemies' pursuit. The narration is relatively unrestricted once Willie reaches the South, moving between him and members of the Canfield family. We usually know more about where they are than Willie does, and the narrative generates suspense by showing them coming toward the places where Willie is hiding.
>
> Specific settings fulfill distinct narrative functions. The McKay "estate," which Willie envisions as a mansion, turns out to be a tumbledown shack.

The McKay place is paralleled to (contrasted with) the Canfields' palatial plantation home. In narrative terms the Canfield home gains even more functional importance when the Canfield father forbids his sons to kill Willie on the premises: "our code of honor forbids us to shoot him while he is a guest in our house." (Once Willie overhears this, he determines never to leave.) Thus, ironically, the home of Willie's enemies becomes the only safe spot in town, and many scenes are organized around the Canfield brothers' attempts to lure Willie out. At the end of the film another setting takes on significance: the meadows, mountains, river banks, rapids, and waterfalls across which the Canfields pursue Willie. Finally, the feud ends back in the Canfield house itself, with Willie now welcomed as the daughter's husband. The pattern of development is clear: from the opening shoot-out at the McKay house that breaks up Willie's home, to the final scene in the Canfield house with Willie becoming part of a new family. In such ways every setting becomes highly motivated by the narrative's system of causes and effects, parallels and contrasts, and overall development. (Bordwell and Thompson 142–43)

COMPOSITION AND THE IMAGE

In any movie, it is the camera that eventually films a mise-en-scène: When you watch a movie, you see not only the setting, actors, and lighting, but all these elements as they are recorded and then projected. The composition of a scene through the film image is what distinguishes film from drama, and it is another important dimension of the movies that a good writer should be able to discuss. When you watch a home video, you might first recognize a party with you and your friends. However, with a closer look, you might also comment on how the images, because of the angles or coloring, make some of those friends look taller or darker than they really are. In the same way, a film image may influence the way you see a scene or a character in that scene. The student who begins by writing, "The scene had three characters..." will seem less attentive and perceptive than the student who begins, "The visual angle on the scene made the three characters appear..." This section considers some of the terminology you can use to discuss these compositional features.

The Shot

The *shot* is the single image you see on the screen before the film cuts to a different image. Unlike a photograph, a single shot can include a variety of action or movement, and the frame that contains the image may even move. One shot may show a cowboy at a bar and then magnify the figure by moving the camera closer. When the image switches to another position and point of view on the cowboy—say, from the opposite side of the bar—the film has cut to a second shot. In writing about film, you should be sensitive to the two primary dimensions of the shot:

- its photographic properties
- its moving frame

The *photographic properties* of a shot are the qualities of the film image that are found in any photograph, plus the speed at which the scene is filmed. These properties include tone, film speed, and the various perspectives created by the image. *Tone* refers to the range and texture of the colors in a film image. A movie such as *The Wizard of Oz* (1939) uses a Technicolor scheme full of primary reds and yellows to suggest a fantasy world very different from the black-and-white Kansas. Some films, such as George Clooney's *Goodnight, and Good Luck* (2005), use black-and-white tones to suggest an older movie genre or past historical period, as Clooney does in his film about Edward R. Murrow's black-and-white television broadcasts of the 1950s. Woody Allen in *Zelig* (1983) tells a story with intentionally grainy black-and-white tones to make parts of his modern movie look like an old documentary, and in *Schindler's List,* Steven Spielberg occasionally disrupts a horrific story in black and white with the fleeting glimpse of a child's bright red coat. Ask if the colors are realistic. If not, why not? Is there a pattern in the way a film uses a particular color or group of colors? Does the film use colors symbolically, as Ingmar Bergman uses red in *Cries and Whispers* (1972) to suggest both violence and passion? If the movie is in black and white, how does the black and white add to the movie, especially if the filmmaker could have used color? How do the colors and tones relate to the themes of the film?

Film speed is the rate at which the film is shot; it is most obvious in instances of slow or fast motion. Action in slow or fast motion usually indicates a change in the nature of what is happening or how the audience is supposed to perceive what is happening. Sometimes, slow motion is used to indicate that the action is part of a character's dream; sometimes, fast motion is a way of commenting comically on a scene—when, for instance, action on an assembly line suddenly moves at superhuman speed. It is easy to note when the speed of the film is no longer normal; be prepared to examine why these moments are singled out by the filmmaker. In Nagisa Oshima's *Merry Christmas, Mr. Lawrence* (1982), David Bowie confronts his Japanese adversary with two kisses that are filmed in slow motion; it is clear that this is Oshima's way of underlining this shattering climax in their relationship. Keep in mind, however, that many older silent movies were filmed and printed at the rate of sixteen frames per second, and their action may look faster when shown at the modern standard of twenty-four frames per second.

The *perspective* of the image refers to the kind of spatial relationship an image establishes between the different objects and figures it is photographing. These different relationships are the products of different kinds of lenses and the way those lenses are used. Thus one movie may constantly present scenes with a great deal of *depth* or *deep focus* so that the audience can see characters in the background as sharply as it sees characters in the foreground. Another movie (often an older one) may wish to isolate or highlight only certain characters or events in the image, and it consequently uses a *shallow focus* that will clearly show only one plane in the image, such as the man with a gun who stands in the foreground apart from the blurry crowd in the background. Much less commonly seen is the odd moment of *rack focus,* when the focus is quickly changed, or pulled, from one figure or object to another within the same shot, as when the image switches focus from the face of a man talking to a piano falling out the window in the background.

Still other kinds of perspective relationships can be used in creating an image, but even while you are learning these other technical terms, you can begin to analyze perspective relationships by asking some basic questions: Who or what is in focus in an image, and why? Do the images create a world with depth, or does that world seem unusually flat? How would you describe the space in a particular image? Is it crowded? Open? Wide? Distorted? When a specific wide-screen image drowns the characters in space, what does this say about them and their world? Make the power of the image itself come alive in your writing. Make the subject of your essays not just what you see, but also how the image makes you see people and things in a certain way and in a certain relationship to one another. Here is an example in which the student briefly looks at color, tone, and spatial relations in Nicolas Roeg's *Don't Look Now* (1973):

N. Singerpanz

Don't Look Now (1973) is a movie about not wanting to see red but being unable not to see red. The story concerns a man and a woman whose young daughter dies tragically by drowning. Later, they go to Venice, where he has a job restoring an old church that is slowly sinking. They both want to forget the horrible death of their daughter, but in Venice, they—and we, the frightened viewers—are pursued by a color, the bright red glow of the raincoat the daughter was wearing when she died.

Even before her death the color leaps out of the film. While the father is studying slides of the church he will repair, the tone and texture of the red in the image begin to vibrate and then ooze like blood. As if it is a premonition, he dashes outside to find his child face down in a pond, her coat the same color as the red in the slide.

Venice is a rather gray city in this movie, but wherever the father turns the bright shade of red seems to catch his eye, as if it has a life of its own or is beckoning from another world. For a second or longer, stained-glass windows, pieces of clothing, or a passing car appear to bear the shade of red which we and he have come to identify with the dead daughter. That red is a common color, if a shocking one, only adds to the mystery and confusion as this simple color grows more and more hypnotic and frightening. It seems to contrast with the ordinary gray life of Venice, and, since visual space is made so claustrophobic by the narrow, windy streets of the city, the glimpses we and the father catch of a fleeing red figure in the background become moments of true terror.

This color becomes a life in itself, a life that comes to mean death. The grays of Venice and the mazelike spaces of its streets make this color impossible to miss and more fascinating because it is always vanishing into the depths. The shock of the final scene, when we and the father finally corner the color, suggests that we have been horribly seduced by the power of Roeg's images.

The *frame* of the movie image forms its border and contains the mise-en-scène. Many movies, such as Jean Renoir's *Grand Illusion* (1937) and Alfred Hitchcock's *Rear Window* (1954), fill their mise-en-scène with the internal frames of windows or doorways or stage sets to call attention to the importance of frames and point of view in the story. Almost every film, though, must maintain a certain consciousness about the frame of the movie screen and the frame of the camera (Figure 3.09). A wide-screen frame is especially suited to catching the open spaces of a western or the vast stellar spaces of sci-fi films. The smaller standard frame is, perhaps, best suited to more personal interior dramas or genres like the melodrama, to which a small frame can contribute a sense of anything from domestic comfort and closeness to claustrophobia. Through the course of a film, there will be a number of other more particular questions to ask about the framing:

- What is the angle at which the camera frame represents the action? Does it create a *high angle,* viewing its subject from above, or a *low angle,* viewing the action from below? When a conversation between two people is shot through a group of alternating high angles and low angles, it could mean that one character is tall and the other is short; it could also say that one of the two is the more dominant personality.
- Does the height of the frame correspond to a normal relationship to the people and objects before the camera; that is, are they at eye level, more or less? Or does the camera seem to be placed

Figure 3.09 What makes this shot from *The Exorcist* (1973) so disturbing?

at an odd height, too high or too low? At the beginning of *Rebel without a Cause* (1955), for instance, the camera is positioned at ground level to capture James Dean's desperate and pathetic embrace of a small toy as he crumbles to the ground.

- Does the camera frame ever seem unbalanced in relation to the space and action (called a *canted frame*)? If so, why does this occur when it does? Is it recreating the perspective of a character looking at the action from an odd angle so that the buildings appear diagonal rather than vertical? Is it meant to recreate the perspective of a drunk, or might it be a more subtle way of commenting, for instance, on a community that lacks harmony and balance?

- What kind of distance does the frame maintain from its subject? Does the film use many close-ups (for instance, showing just the characters' faces), medium shots (showing most of a character's body), or long shots (showing full bodies from a distance)? Perhaps a scene uses a series of these shots, beginning with a long shot of a man on the street, then showing a medium shot of him looking in a store window, and concluding with a close-up of his surprised face as he sees something in the window. Does the movie develop a more elaborate combination of these that might be interpreted according to some meaningful pattern: close-ups for love scenes and long shots for battle scenes, for instance?

- Besides describing and containing the action, does the frame suggest other action or space outside its borders? Do important events or sounds occur outside the borders of the frame—in *offscreen space*? What is the significance of this offscreen space or its relation to what is seen within the frame? Is offscreen space used for comic effect, as in Buster Keaton's movie *The General* (1927), in which we discover that the wheel he is sitting on is part of a train located outside the frame and about to move? Or does it have a serious meaning, as in Robert Bresson's films, in which offscreen space suggests a type of spiritual reality his characters are unable to grasp or understand because it is literally beyond the frame of their world?

Within one scene, any of these compositions may change as the camera creates a *moving frame* by altering its position in relation to the object being filmed. A romantic close-up of two lovers whispering, for example, may suddenly change its meaning if the camera frame moves backward and makes them part of a long shot full of spectators: What was at first romantic has become, through the movement of the frame, comic. This kind of framing action, called *reframing*, can be done in ways that rely entirely on the movement of the frame, not on the editing of images through cuts (see pp. 64–70).

When the frame moves to high, overhead *crane shots,* which look down on the action, we all realize there has been a dramatic change in perspective: The film may be emphasizing the smallness of the character in relation to the rest of his or her space, or it may be revealing other action, such as the approach of the cavalry on the other side of the mountain range. When the frame moves up and down, *tilting* from one position, it may simply be following the point of view of a character who is looking up and down, but it may also be a way of making a statement about high and low objects (about, for instance, the tourist who feels overwhelmed by the skyscrapers of New York City). Another kind of mobile frame is the *pan,* in which the frame moves from side to side without a change in the position of the camera or the point from which the scene is viewed: Surveying the street before him, a character may look slowly from left to right, and the camera may pan to recreate the continuous movement of his gaze. In contrast, a *tracking* or *dolly shot* is not stationary but follows or intrudes on the action by moving the position of the camera (often on small tracks) and thus taking the frame forward, backward, or around the subject. During a cocktail-party scene, the film may recreate the roving intimacy of the gathering by using a dolly shot that follows a character through the crowd. If this action is achieved by a *handheld shot,* in which the camera is carried by the camera operator, the shot may be jerkier (and may, in some ways, seem more realistic).

Since frames imply a perspective on the world or on certain characters, their mobility or lack of it can point to the very foundation of the world you see in those frames. Is it an active world you are seeing, or one that seems rigid and static? The complexities of that world are often revealed as the frames move and change, and the more exactly you can note these frames, the more incisive your analysis will be. Try, at some point, to base your analysis of a character or a situation exclusively on the framing action that describes them. What patterns can you see? Does this character always look at the world through close-ups that track through crowds and situations, without ever getting a larger perspective on them? Does that consistent way of framing the action suggest that he participates but never really sees the whole picture?

Remember that frames and their actions have no universal meaning. Just as colors do not have unchanging symbolic value, camera angles and movements do not have to mean the same thing in different movies. Low-angle shots do not always signify dominance, nor do high-angle shots always suggest oppression (as is sometimes thought). Although in one movie a low-angle shot may remind the viewer that a weak character is being looked at by a stronger, more dangerous person, in another movie that low-angle shot may be used to describe the wonder of a child looking at a person she loves. If you begin by noting visual details carefully, you can reflect on how particular framing actions work in specific films and on how they provoke certain questions about those films and their themes. An endless series of close-ups means one thing in a movie made for American television, where it may underline the importance of the individual character, and another thing in a European art film, where it may suggest the unknowable quality of the human face. In an Ozu film, the low height of the director's frame may be meant to suggest the more relaxed, meditative perspective of a Japanese person looking at the world from the floor of a tatami room, but the Belgian filmmaker Chantal Akerman claims that the low height of her frames occurs because she is short! The lesson should be clear: Don't simply describe technical details and expect them to be self-explanatory. Rather, put them to work to convey an idea about the various ways that frames and their points of view operate and what they mean in specific films, in specific cultures, and at specific times.

The Edited Image

In the simplest sense, editing is the linking of two different shots (in older films the product of splicing together two different pieces of film but today produced by linking different digital images). Usually, the editing follows some logic of development (an image of a woman and then the object she is looking at, for example) or is meant to make a statement of some sort (an image of an egotistical czar and then one of a peacock). Recall the cowboy at the bar: When a long shot shows him at the bar and then slowly tracks in closer to capture him close up, this is reframing within a single shot. But if, after that first image, the camera stops and moves to another position (maybe a low angle on the other side of the bar), that reframed long shot has now been edited into two shots. The break between the two images is a *cut*.

A shot can be held on the screen for any length of time, the result being a certain *editing pace* or *rhythm*. Because the pace of the editing is relative, we should try to note why and how a film or part of a film is edited according to a certain rhythm. We expect a chase scene to be rapidly edited (with lots of quick cuts and brief shots), but to make us comically aware of our expectations about editing, that chase scene could be edited with very slow rhythms and few cuts. As an exercise, observe exactly how long a single image remains on the screen in any movie and then reflect on why the filmmaker cuts to another angle or image at that point. Does the director use mostly *long takes,* shots that remain on a scene or object for an unusually long time (as Terrence Malick did in *The Thin Red Line* [1999] when he held the image on grassy fields or the branches of trees for mystically long periods)? Or does the film cut rapidly from one image to another, as in chase sequences in *The Bourne Ultimatum* (2007)? Does the pace of the editing change with the scene, for example, by using quick cuts on the streets and slow, long takes inside the home?

In the larger sense, *editing* refers to how shots are built into larger pieces of a movie and, hence, larger units of meaning. A series of shots can thus be carefully joined to create a single *scene,* which is usually an action confined to one place and time: for example, in Jane Campion's *The Piano* (1993), the scene in which Ada (Holly Hunter) arrives on a remote beach in nineteenth-century New Zealand, or, in *The Battleship Potemkin* (1925), the scene in which the officers inspect the rotten meat. The latter begins with a group of angry sailors gathered on deck around a piece of maggot-infested meat; the ship's surgeon inspects the meat, which is shown in close-up, and announces that the maggots are simply dead flies; the scene ends as another officer disperses the outraged sailors.

When these shots describe significantly more action and more time and more than one location, the interwoven and unified group of shots or scenes that results is often called a *sequence.* In *The Piano,* the beach scene becomes part of a larger arrival sequence when Ada is met and led through the jungle to her future home; in *The Battleship Potemkin,* the scenes that dramatize the sailors' mounting discontent make those scenes part of a complicated sequence leading to their rebellion. As part of the previous exercise, see if you can now mark off sections of a film that show how shots can be edited into complex relationships that create unified scenes or sequences.

Most of us pay little conscious attention to editing because we know and enjoy most the *continuity editing* of classical cinema. This editing style is appropriately called *invisible editing,* because the filmmaker, not wanting the editing to distract from the story, avoids cuts and transitions between images that would be too obvious. Through various means, the filmmaker attempts to hide the film editing so that we view the images as a continuous picture. Thus, even though *The Maltese Falcon* (1941) is a very skillfully and stylishly edited movie—carefully balancing Sam Spade's entrances and exits and his keen method of noticing the details in a room—we view it as a continuous action in which obtrusive cuts would seem out of place.

Yet, continuity editing depends on some highly crafted editing techniques, techniques that, when analyzed, reveal important points about the characters and story. *Establishing shots,* for instance, are the shots that begin a scene or sequence as a way of locating a scene clearly in a certain place before dividing that sequence into more detailed shots. *Casablanca* (1942) begins with a series of establishing shots that describe the city on the map, the kind of people in the city, and, finally, the outside of Rick's cabaret. Only then does the film move inside to begin its story about Rick. The *shot/reverse-shot,* or *shot/countershot,* pattern is also a fundamental part of continuity editing. With this technique, an exchange between two characters (or a character and an object) is edited to appear logical and natural by cutting from the person speaking or looking to the object or person being addressed or seen; for instance, a shot shows Humphrey Bogart asking Ingrid Bergman a question and then cuts to her responding. When considering a film that uses continuity editing, a writer can begin, as with realism itself, by questioning the basic purposes of the techniques used:

- Are there larger implications concerning the world and society in the "continuity"? Is the movie trying to create a sense of a logical or safe world? Do establishing shots, for instance, indicate that the characters (and the audience) know where they are and should feel at home? Does the continuity help establish, as in *The Philadelphia Story* (1940), a sense of logical inevitability, a feeling that events and relationships have to move toward a natural conclusion, that Hepburn and Grant will remarry?
- Has the continuity editing been adjusted to fit a genre or to create certain emotional responses? Do road movies have fewer cuts and more long takes? In westerns, do the shot/reverse-shot patterns involve people and things more than people and other people?
- When the editing presents a fundamentally continuous and unified world, are there times when that continuity is disrupted? If so, why? In *The Lady from Shanghai* (1947), for instance, Orson Welles regularly disrupts the viewer's sense of space and time through the questionable reliability of the narrator, O'Hara, and through visual distortions, such as in the hall of mirrors at the end of the movie. In this case, the disrupting images and editing imply the collapse of a world incapable of maintaining old certainties.
- Does the shot/reverse-shot pattern in a particular sequence tell you anything about the characters involved or how they see the world and each other? Are considerably more shots given to one person or the other? Does the editing create a pattern in which one character's eyes never meet the other's?

- How would you distinguish between the continuity editing of an older, classic movie like *Scarface* (1932) and that of a more modern Hollywood film like *Salt* (2010)? Does one use more long takes and the other more quick cuts? How would you differentiate between the continuity editing in a European movie such as *The Rules of the Game* (1939) and an American movie of the same period such as *The Grapes of Wrath* (1940)? Does the first rely more on a moving frame to emphasize the world around the characters and the second more on smooth editing techniques that emphasize the characters themselves?

Continuity editing can also use more noticeable and stylized methods, which are often associated with older movies. These include the following:

- *Fade-in* or *fade-out:* An image is darkened or lightened so that it appears or disappears.
- *Iris-in* or *iris-out:* The new image appears as an expanding circle in the middle of the old image, or the old image becomes a contracting circle that disappears into the new image.
- *Wipe:* A line moves across an image to gradually clear one shot and introduce another.
- *Dissolve:* A new shot is briefly superimposed on the fading old shot.

When these techniques are used in a movie, ask what they are meant to achieve. Used in older movies, they create logical transitions from one time or place to another. In a D. W. Griffith film, a fade might be saying, "Later that same day," as the shot reveals the same kitchen in the evening; a wipe could suggest, "In another part of town," when the interior of the courthouse is wiped off by a line across the image and a Chinese opium den appears on the other side of the line. When watching an older film, ask if one technique is used for one kind of linkage (a wipe connecting different places, for example) and another technique for other situations (a dissolve indicating changes in time). When analyzing modern movies, ask why the editor would choose these older continuity devices. Does Woody Allen use irises just for a humorous effect because they are so unusual in a contemporary movie? In *The Cotton Club* (1984), are the wipes simply a reference to the 1920s, when the story takes place, or are they a dramatic means of emphasizing the passage of time and history— one of the main themes of the film?

Besides recognizing the techniques of continuity editing, you should learn to recognize, make sense of, and analyze how films undermine or challenge your expectations about continuity editing. Especially in more contemporary films, begin to notice when a film breaks with the standards of continuity editing and begin to ask questions such as the following:

- Why are there so few establishing shots in a particular movie? Is it difficult to say where an action takes place because the scene begins with a close-up of a character or inside an unidentified room? Do the characters seem to share our disorientation? Is this disorientation related to the themes of the film?
- Why is the temporal continuity within a film broken up in such a confusing fashion? Does the editing use a number of *jump cuts,* in which a continuous shot is suddenly broken and the image jumps to new figures or another background or even the same background but at a different time? As a character discusses her life, for instance, the monologue may be broken in places, while the light in the room changes with each jump cut to indicate the passage of time. Is the filmmaker trying to make us more aware of the passage of time, or is he or she commenting ironically on this character's boring life story?
- Why is there no point of view with which we can identify? Does this have something to do with the lack of shot/reverse-shot scenes that would allow us to identify with the perspective of a character? Does the filmmaker, as Werner Herzog often does in his films, force his audience to remain detached from the ordinary people and to identify instead with animals, lunatics, or dwarfs? Does the film contain images that seem to have no place in the story? A movie about war may inexplicably cut to an image of a cherry tree, time and time again. Is it a symbol? Is it part of a character's memory? Why is the continuity of the action broken by this unexplained image?

In these cases, the editing calls attention to itself, and the trade-off for that obtrusiveness is an initial confusion about why the editing has upset the usual perception of the world. When that confusion leads to larger questions (and, perhaps, to answers) about the themes and the historical context of the film, the writer is beginning to sketch a paper topic. After thinking about a Herzog movie, one student realized his paper would discuss how Herzog's unconventional editing, particularly his undermining of a shot/reverse-shot exchange, is part of an effort to move the audience outside the logical patterns that have traditionally placed human society at the center of the world, part of Herzog's vision of a natural world that is more important than individual men and women.

In recent decades, editing has entered the digital age, leaving behind the older, more laborious, and more expensive processes of editing images by hand on a Moviola or later on a flatbed editing table. Now editing is almost exclusively accomplished through computer-based nonlinear digital editing systems. With *digital nonlinear editing*, images are stored on the hard drives of high-capacity computers so that editors of movies today can quickly and easily access both sound bits and images and combine and recombine those in different relationships. Digital filmmaking theoretically allows a shot to last an almost unlimited amount of time and can create the kind of nonstop immediacy and randomness seen in a film such as the 2008 *Cloverfield*, a fictional movie about a monster's invasion of New York City recorded on a character's digital camera. Besides these fairly obvious effects, consider other ways nonlinear digital editing can shape a film. Has digital editing created new relationships between music and image in some contemporary films? Has the longer duration of the digital image encouraged more creative and dynamic compositions within the frame rather than between edited frames? How has digital filmmaking and editing impacted recent documentaries?

When examining both traditional and contemporary editing strategies and the relationships between shots, begin with some general guidelines about what to look for but adapt them to deal with concrete and specific uses and variations in each film.

First, observe how the editing of the shots establishes certain relationships between the objects and actions. Does the editing establish connections or oppositions among the people, things, and actions being shown? In *The Last Laugh* (1924), the doorman is frequently linked to the image of the revolving door, and the identification of the two predicts the reversal of the man's good fortune. In *2001: A Space Odyssey* (1968), a prehistoric ape tosses a bone into the air, which then becomes the image of a spaceship. This famous *match-on-action*—two images being edited together as parallel actions or motions—crystallizes thousands of years of human development propelled by violence and the need to conquer people and territory.

Second, accustom yourself to noticing more abstract relationships between images. This is a more difficult practice, but, as the example from Eisenstein's *The Battleship Potemkin* shows (see pp. 28–33), these more abstract aspects of editing can be brilliantly used for certain effects. Does the direction and movement of the figures in the different images match when these shots are connected, creating, for example, a kind of visual and emotional force driving in a single direction? Are graphic contrasts or similarities created through the use of space in the different shots, for example, by alternating large and small spaces? Does the editing set up certain rhythms by strictly controlling the length of each shot? (Although most of us know best the accelerated rhythms of a chase sequence, the editing can fashion many other kinds of rhythms.) Remember, these formal patterns have no final and universal meaning in themselves, and their evolution through film history is not independent of other historical questions. Although editing can be seen as a formal way of organizing images in time and space, more than just formal or technical issues are usually involved. Look precisely at editing, but let it lead you to think more about how and what films mean. In the following student essay, the writer examined a very short sequence in *Citizen Kane* (1941) and related the editing and the composition of the image to a specific theme:

Scott Richardson

Editing Breakfast in *Citizen Kane*

Soon after Charles Foster Kane marries Emily, the woman of his dreams who is brought back from Europe like one of his statues, their marriage begins to collapse. The severity and intensity of this collapse are captured in one two-minute sequence, which remains one of the most striking examples of Welles's evocative and economical editing in *Citizen Kane.*

The sequence begins with a medium two-shot of Kane and Emily in relatively warm light. Their conversation is teasing and intimate, visually reinforced by a shot/reverse-shot exchange of loving looks: He tells her she is beautiful, and when she complains about his having to leave for his newspaper office, he says he will call and change his appointments. That exchange is followed by five more short shot/reverse-shot pairs, and in each, the eyes of the couple grow increasingly suspicious and severe. The conversations are progressively hostile and clipped, and the newspaper becomes both a visual and a verbal symbol of their growing division. In the first scene of this middle section, she complains, "Charles, if I didn't trust you....What do you do on a newspaper in the middle of the night?" In the third, Emily pleads with him to stop attacking her uncle, the president, in his newspaper. By the fifth, he is not even allowing her to finish her sentence:

EMILY: Really, Charles, people have a right to expect....

CHARLES: What I care to give them.

Through the entire sequence, the changes in the clothing and other aspects of the mise-en-scène indicate that the passage of time is also a passage away from emotional intimacy. Kane changes from a romantic tuxedo to a business suit. Their setting alters from an unobstructed and close space to an obstructed space cluttered with plants, flowers, and newspapers.

The succinct logic of the editing is then powerfully concluded with a shot/reverse-shot and then another two-shot. In the shot/reverse-shot, the eyes no longer meet or match, since they are now both reading separate newspapers—he, his own (*The Inquirer*), she, the rival (*The Chronicle*). Formally balancing the opening of the sequence, the medium-long two-shot has much colder and darker lighting. The two former lovers are placed conspicuously at opposite sides of the frame.

The real time that this sequence describes is probably many years. Yet, through a rigorous and creative use of an edited space and a series of conversations within that space, Welles depicts more than just the synopsis of a failed marriage. Linking the six encounters, appropriately, with flash pans, he also tells a succinct and cinematic version of the entire tale of *Citizen Kane:* of how Kane's greatest desires seem to turn to dust almost immediately after he achieves them and of how he consequently becomes a man always alienated in the great spaces that surround him.

SOUND

In the 1992 *White Men Can't Jump,* two basketball-playing buddies— Sidney (Wesley Snipes) and Billy (Woody Harrelson)—listen to a Jimi Hendrix tune on their car radio. Although they are both listening attentively, Sidney scolds Billy by pointing out, "You're listening, but you're not hearing it." In a similar sense, many moviegoers listen to films but in most cases have not learned to hear them. What this common failure means to new and curious students of the movies is that many topics and problems having to do with film sound have only recently begun to be addressed and are waiting for good ears to take them up. If students with an interest in music and sound direct and concentrate that interest on a movie or a specific group of movies, they will tackle some original and provocative material.

Keep in mind that for over thirty years, until 1927, silent films obviously did not have the technological resources to develop *synchronous sound* that could record and match sound with the filmed image. In fact, however, these so-called silent films were surrounded by orchestral and other musical accompaniments and sound effects in the theater. Not only do these films sometimes have complex relationships between the images and the scores that accompanied them, but they also offer students rich analytical opportunities in exploring the creative ways that (1) sound and silence can be implied or suggested and (2) intertitles adapt literary descriptions and dialogue to film.

In theory, sound can be used and edited with as much complexity and intelligence as images can. Certainly, sound has many dimensions and uses in film. It can be described according to pitch, loudness, or timbre; it can figure in a film as *direct sound* (recorded when the image is being shot) or *postdubbed sound* (sound and dialogue added later in the studio). Movie sound can take the form of dialogue, music, or noise (thunder or a car screeching to a halt), any or all of these sounds being naturally or artificially produced. Film sound can have a multitude of relations to the image and the narrative: most broadly, its source may be an object or action in the image, thus as *onscreen or synchronous sound*, or its source may be outside the film frame as *offscreen or asynchronous sound*. Whether offscreen or onscreen, *diegetic sound* has its source in the narrative world of the film (such as when a character breaks into song), while *nondiegetic sound* has its source outside that world (such as in the background music of an orchestral score during a romantic scene). It can even precede or follow the image to which it is linked as a *sound bridge* (when a character's remark, for example, forms a bridge into the next image).

As with the analysis of visual details in a film, a precise vocabulary and terminology always advance the analysis of film sound, and some useful technical terms for discussing film sound include the following:

- *Sound continuity* describes the scoring and mixing of sound to create a unified atmosphere or tone in a scene or sequence.

- *Sound montage* composes different pieces of sound to create disjunctions and unexpected relations between those sounds.
- *Ambient sound* describes the background noises or music that surround the main action and dialogue.
- *Overlapping dialogue* is a simultaneous mixing and overlapping of characters' speech.
- *Voice-off* originates in a speaker who was or will be seen onscreen but is not at the time the voice is heard.
- *Voice-over* is the voice of a narrator or commentator who typically is not part of the story or diegesis and cannot be heard by the characters. In conventional documentaries, this transcendent voice is often referred to as "the voice of God."
- *Narrative cueing* is the use of a sound or piece of music to support a moment or motif in the story, such as a romantic violin motif when two characters meet. When these cues are sudden and especially dramatic, they are sometimes called *stingers.*

Throughout film history, one can find movies in which the sound alone would make a major topic for analysis. A well-known example, Jean-Marie Straub and Danièle Huillet's *The Chronicle of Anna Magdalena Bach* (1968), sets up a complex opposition between the graceful music of Bach on the sound track and the tormented story of Bach's physical and financial troubles. Francis Coppola's *The Conversation* (1974) recounts the story of a man who specializes in sound surveillance, who tries to discover the truth through sound alone, and who finally loses all faith in the visual world. Some of the most fascinating and provocative uses of sound are found in films of the early 1930s, when sound was first being introduced into the movies. In one early sound film, *The Thirty-Nine Steps* (1935), Hitchcock employs sound as a central element in the plot: At a critical moment, he creates a dramatic *sound match* by connecting a woman's scream and the whistle of a locomotive to link disparate images (Figures 3.10 and 3.11).

To write about sound, one must first learn to attend to sound—truly to hear it. This does not mean that the more obvious or dramatic uses of sound in film—in movies with the lavish and complex sound tracks found in Paul Thomas Anderson's *There Will Be Blood* (2007) or in films organized around musical performances like *Shine a Light* (2008), Martin Scorsese's concert film about the Rolling Stones—cannot inspire good essays. They certainly can. But because a good essay is one that reveals intuitive, careful, and discriminating thinking, a good essay on sound will often attend to what might normally escape a normal viewer and listener.

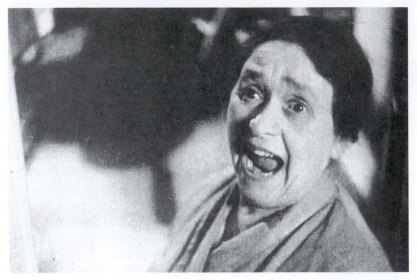

Figure 3.10 *The Thirty-Nine Steps* (1935): creating transitions and links...

A writer about sound in film might therefore begin by bluntly asking the following:

- What is the relation of the sound to the image in specific scenes or sequences? How might the answer to that question be refined to reveal the aims, achievements, or even failures of sound in the movie?
- Is the sound used to link images, or does the sound have the conventional role of beginning and terminating with the image?
- Does sound ever become more important than the image, and what is the reason for this unusual strategy?
- Do the musical numbers in a musical have any special relation to the narrative structure (for instance, do they occur when the characters need to escape into fantasy)?
- Why does the dialogue of the characters overlap or seem mumbled in some recent movies so that it is difficult to understand the characters? Does the dialogue serve some other purpose than to help tell the story?
- What role does silence play in this movie?
- Are there sound motifs that identify the characters or actions?
- Does the rhythm of the sound support or serve as counterpoint to the rhythm of the editing?
- If you had to pick three key sound sequences from this movie, which would they be, and why?

Figure 3.11 ...through sound matches.

These questions are only a sample of the many inquiries that movie sound and particular movies might inspire. Listen to all film sound and write about it with the same curiosity and suspicion exhibited by the characters in Godard's *Every Man for Himself* (1980), who continually hear background music and wonder where it's coming from and why. Here a renowned French filmmaker (and early innovator with sound), René Clair, writing in 1929, detailed one of the first successes with sound in the cinema:

> Of all the films now showing in London, *Broadway Melody* is having the greatest success. This new American film represents the sum total of all the progress achieved in sound films since the appearance of *The Jazz Singer* two years ago. For anyone who has some knowledge of the complicated technique of sound recording, this film is a marvel. Harry Beaumont, the director, and his collaborators (of whom there are about fifteen, mentioned by name in the credit titles, quite apart from the actors) seem to delight in playing with all the difficulties of visual and sound recording. The actors move, walk, run, talk, shout, and whisper, and their movements and voices are reproduced with a flexibility which would seem miraculous if we did not know that science and meticulous organization have many other miracles in store for us. In this film, nothing is left to chance. Its makers have worked with the precision of engineers, and their achievement is a lesson to those who still imagine that the creation of a film can take place under conditions of chaos known as inspiration.

In *Broadway Melody,* the talking film has for the first time found an appropriate form: it is neither theater nor cinema, but something altogether new. The immobility of planes, that curse of talking films, has gone. The camera is as mobile, the angles are as varied as in a good silent film. The acting is first-rate, and Bessie Love talking manages to surpass the silent Bessie Love whom we so loved in the past. The sound effects are used with great intelligence, and if some of them still seem superfluous, others deserve to be cited as examples.

For instance, we hear the noise of a door being slammed and a car driving off while we are shown Bessie Love's anguished face watching from a window the departure which we do not see. This short scene in which the whole effect is concentrated on the actress's face, and which the silent cinema would have had to break up in several visual fragments, owes its excellence to the "unity of place" achieved through sound. In another scene we see Bessie Love lying thoughtful and sad; we feel that she is on the verge of tears; but her face disappears in the shadow of a fade-out, and from the screen, now black, emerges a single sob.

In these two instances the sound, at an opportune moment, has replaced the shot. It is by this economy of means that the sound film will most probably secure original effects. (93–94)

ANIMATION, 3-D, AND NEW MEDIA

In recent years and as part of the larger digital revolution, new media and new technologies have become a major part of film and media cultures that extend or cross the borders of traditional narrative cinema. While animated films have been a part of film history since its beginning, to take one important example, digital animation processes developed and refined in the last fifteen years have generated a renaissance of animated movies—from *Toy Story* (1995) to *Megamind* (2010)—capable of creating more elaborate and sophisticated images than ever before. One result of the expanding vision of animated cinema has been the development of narratives with bi-level addresses whose stories can speak at once to children and adults, especially apparent in Japanese anime films such as the two *Ghost in the Shell* films (1996, 2004). Yet, whether aimed mainly at children or at adults (as, for instance in the 2008 animated documentary *Waltz with Bashir*), animated films elicit these first questions with which to begin an analysis:

- If the film straddles the world of children and adults, how does this overlapping take shape in the film and how does it develop unique themes and perspectives on the world? About the role of imagination? About the nature of reality?

• How and why does animation complicate the relations between the human world and the nonhuman world in the film as a function of its forms and themes?

More recently, and most famously announced by James Cameron's *Avatar* (2009), 3-D has become the latest technological innovation in a long history of special effects that extends back through Georges Méliès's 1902 *Trip to the Moon* and through early experiments with 3-D in the 1950s. Thanks to the remarkable advances in digital and computer programs and equipment in recent years, movies can now be filmed in 3-D (although many recent films feature only postproduction enhancements) and even the most unlikely films, such as *Saw 3D* (2010) or *Jackass 3-D* (2010), attempt to take advantage of an often astonishing realism that allows spectators to experience a film as if physically inhabiting it. As with older special effects, however, students should immediately ask some fundamental questions of 3-D: To what extent do the special effects add significantly to the themes of the narrative and our understanding of the film? To what extent is 3-D merely window dressing?

Finally and perhaps most important, the digital revolution has begun to dramatically change how we view movies. Not only are people watching more movies through the Internet, CD-ROMs, or iPods, but more and more art and information is being created to be seen and understood specifically through these new media vehicles. If you have the desire or opportunity to write about these kinds of new media products, consider these questions as a starting point:

• How do the images, stories, or sounds emphasize, more than traditional films or videos, a unique interactivity between them and the viewer? How does that help explain their aims and goals?

• How is the technology of the particular media part of its message?

In observing and writing about any formal features of a film or new technologies delivering films, your first goal should be to achieve as much precision as possible. Developing a vocabulary of technical terms can be extremely helpful, but most important is developing the ability to write concrete descriptions of images and sounds in the way that best allows your reader to see and hear the images and sounds you are describing. Sometimes, of course, that detailed precision is more difficult to accomplish than at other times. When you must work with only sketchy notes, try to get as much out of those notes as possible. There is nothing wrong with writing about a general style in a film ("a predominance of long shots," "an amplified sound track," or "exaggeratedly artificial sets"), as long as your paper has a focus that does not rely solely on generalities. Otherwise, always try to integrate as much accurate concrete description as possible into your argument. As practice, describe—without analyzing—all the technical features of an opening or closing sequence of a movie or an especially interesting use of sound in a scene.

Interpretation, analysis, and evaluation are, however, the primary goals of most writing about film these days. Your appreciation of these elements of a film and how they work together must, at some point, be assimilated and made part of your ideas about what the film or films mean. Whether you examine the editing of a sequence, the lighting throughout a series of films, or how the mise-en-scène, framing, and sound work together in a single scene, remember that seeing, listening, and thinking must join forces as you begin to put your perceptions into words.

SAMPLE ESSAY

This student essay on *The Searchers* (1956) is a good example of how a discriminating analysis involves comparative questions (about film and literature) and, in the process, demonstrates how the movie uses specific technical and formal strategies to express its themes.

book used as framing device
towards beginning and end

Richard Geschke

The Darkened Doorways of *The Searchers*

Based on a 1954 novel by Alan LeMay, John Ford's 1956 adaptation of *The Searchers* dramatizes some of the critical changes that

gives a bit
of background
and has an
argument
in the thesis

can occur in moving a story from a book to the screen. Most film adaptations require some adjustments to the plot (usually deletions). But in Ford's *The Searchers,* we witness a major alteration in the central character, Ethan Edwards, which in turn affects the significance of the entire story. As part of Ford's transformation of Edwards, the film uses a specific image pattern based on the composition of a darkened doorway, an image pattern that indicates how a film narrative can sometimes supplement or even surpass a literary narrative.

Thesis

Although most of the central plot elements remain intact, the most significant change in the adaptation is the character of Ethan

¶ 1.5

Edwards. In the novel he is a fairly traditional western hero who, without much psychological complexity, rescues his niece and returns home. In the film, however, his character grows much more complicated in three ways. First, from the beginning, there is the subtle but definite indication of a mysterious and possibly criminal past: Since the end of the Civil War, Ethan apparently resisted returning home and possibly participated in some unmentionably dangerous, violent, or illegal acts. Second, Ford's Ethan struggles with the turbulent dangers of sexual desire. As carefully suggested by the opening sequence with Ethan and his brother's wife Martha, Ethan has had to repress his love and passion for Martha, presumably knowing that passion would violate the domestic and family codes he lives by. Third, in the film, Ethan is clearly a racist. Unlike in the novel, here he makes sarcastic remarks about his "half-breed" nephew (who is partly Native American) and, more importantly, his mission to find Debbie is, unlike in the novel, motivated by the wish to kill her because he believes she has been sexually violated by her non-white captor.

[handwritten margin note: he does a good job of explaining how Ethan's character has changed and how that changed the story]

A violent, racist, and sexually troubled Ethan thus motivates and complicates the straightforward plot of the novel in new ways. On the one hand, *The Searchers* proceeds as a linear quest: Ethan and Marty Pauley search for the lost Debbie, who has been kidnapped by the Comanche tribe of Scar. That plot is ultimately resolved, in a classical manner, when they find her and she is returned home. A counter-current within this linear, forward plot, however, is an interior search that seems to move backward and inward in the film, investigating Ethan's twisted mind and dark past. At the center of these parallel plots, Marty becomes more and more aware of Ethan's violence and racism, and increasingly confronts him, eventually attempting to stop him from killing Debbie. At first, Ethan does not appear to respond to any of these demands for self-knowledge, and his climactic confrontation with

[handwritten margin note: T.S.]

[handwritten margin note: tells how new Ethan has changed plot]

Scar suggests that nothing about him has changed: He not only kills the Comanche chief but, in an act of grotesque brutality, Ford has this cinematic Ethan actually scalp Scar (which does not happen in the novel).

When in a scene that immediately follows, Ethan chases down Debbie but does not kill her, the film indicates, however, that something has indeed changed in Ethan, that his search for Debbie has revealed something horrid about himself to himself. Perhaps the scalping of Scar, who more and more seems a reflection of Ethan, has acted as a cathartic confrontation with his own dark soul. Perhaps his entire quest has, with the help of Marty, allowed him to see his own barbaric and primitive self. His decision to spare Debbie's life becomes then, at least in part, a decision to acknowledge and free himself from his own violent desires and troubled past. Driven by the need to restore a home and domestic life, Ethan's narrative has now become an inquiry into the dark passions that threaten that home life from within.

Brilliantly dramatizing the tension between Ethan's two searches is a pattern of shots focused on darkened entryways. At the opening, a three-quarters shot from behind Martha shows her looking across the plain as she stands in a doorway. The black interior of the cabin contrasts sharply with the bright light that fills the doorway from outside. A tracking shot then follows Martha out onto the porch where she watches Ethan riding toward her in the distance. At the conclusion, virtually the same shot recurs as Ethan delivers Debbie to her new home with the Jorgensens. After Debbie and the Jorgensens enter the black interior, the newly married Marty and his wife follow. Ethan, though, hesitates on the porch and then turns back into the desert.

Both these shots position Ethan as a wanderer separated from the domestic interiors that he approaches. Complicating this image, moreover, those interiors are blackened in a way that suggests a darker reality than is usually associated with the inside of a home. In an important sense, I believe, the exteriors represent that wild and primitive world that Ethan must wander through, while the interiors of home (and self) represent for Ethan the shadowy and dangerous passion now associated with his illicit love of Martha.

[handwritten margin note: Tells us how the two shots can be interpreted and is explaining the thesis.]

Between these two scenes of darkened doorways is a third scene whose black space acts as the turning point in Ethan's story and a measure of what has changed between the beginning and end of this narrative. After killing Scar, Ethan chases the fleeing Debbie to a cave. Shot from the interior as a medium long shot, the composition here clearly replicates the doorway shots that open and close the film. After approaching the cringing Debbie, Ethan does not, as we expect, kill her but instead lifts her up and says "Let's go home, Debbie." As part of a climactic turning point that begins with his brutal scalping of Scar, the scene becomes a moment of partial and temporary redemption for Ethan as he enters that darkened interior but quietly refuses to act out his repressed violence. When he releases Debbie later at a similar threshold, Ethan has recognized his own violent passion and has resisted it. As he turns at the threshold and walks back into the desert, the long take becomes an acknowledgement that Ethan cannot enter that domestic world because of who he is. In the words of the sound track, he is a man who must continue to "search his heart and soul."

[handwritten margin note: T.S.]

[handwritten margin note: Another scene to support thesis and show how Ethan has resisted his violent side.]

There may be many social or personal reasons for these altera-tions in adapting the novel to the film in this way. What is clear is that Ford's version of the story is a much more troubling and disturbing version as it injects race and sexuality into a character and the narrative. In this case adapting a literary narrative as a film narrative becomes not simply the translation of characters and themes but the creation of significantly different characters and themes.

[handwritten margin note: basically concludes that he created a completely different story from the book]

Exercises

1. Examine a specific sequence from a film that adapts its material from another medium (a novel, a video game). In one or two paragraphs, argue how the adaptation has used its particular technological and formal resources to alter or enhance the original.

2. Focusing on one film, write two or three paragraphs on a single element associated with a specific compositional feature—such as the use of a certain angle in composing shots or a recurrent use of a prop or lighting technique. Conclude by arguing its importance to an understanding of the film.

4

SIX APPROACHES TO WRITING ABOUT FILM

Two writers may both be interested in the lighting in Fritz Lang's *Scarlet Street* (1945), but they may use different methods to focus that discussion. A writer using a formalist approach might analyze the repetitions of an image or the variations of light and shadow within the film; a writer using a historical approach might show how those lighting patterns can be linked to Lang's beginnings in the German expressionist period. Likewise, different approaches are used when writers discuss stylistic similarities in the films of Renoir or historical changes in the musical. In the first case, the writer uses, implicitly, an "auteur" approach, which is based on the belief that films can be linked through the style of the director; in the second, the writer practices genre criticism, which presumes certain accepted types of movies. An awareness of these methods implies a more theoretical aim in your writing than many competent writers about film have (or even wish to have). Yet even when you analyze a single film, it is important and useful to understand the approach you are using, because this awareness will help you to identify the limits of the approach, the needs of your audience, and the goals of the essay.

As you consider a topic for an essay—such as an editing technique—and as you begin to give that topic shape, consider also the assumptions that underlie your approach: Are you interested in a particular technique, such as parallel editing, because one director uses it regularly? Are you interested in examining a series of images because they relate the film to sociological and cultural issues, as Lotte Eisner does when she suggests that the many staircases in German films of the 1920s relate to the romantic ambitions of the society of Weimar Germany? Do you want to focus on how the use of a technique, such as Eisenstein's montage, challenged the way editing had traditionally been used and thus suggests an important change in film form? No matter what approach you find appropriate, you will always clarify your aims and limits if you get a sense of the larger issues. When comparing two films or parts of films, for example, deciding on the terms of that comparison—formal, historical, or other—can be an important step in organizing that comparison.

The following introduction to the major approaches or methods used in writing about film does not attempt to review the complexities of any single approach or the ways two or more approaches may overlap in one study. These sketches and examples should, however, help you to identify approaches that can direct your writing about film and give you a sense of how a particular method might organize and use information.

FILM HISTORY

A historical approach is one of the most widely used methods in film criticism. It can be employed with varying degrees of emphasis or consciousness, but in general, the writer using this approach organizes and investigates films according to their place within a historical context and in light of historical developments. Such an approach might explore the following:

- The historical relationships of the films themselves, as when a writer compares and contrasts the use of sets in a film from the 1930s with their use in a film from the 1970s.
- The relationship of films to their conditions of production, perhaps allowing a writer to make connections between American films of the 1980s and the trend during those years toward the ownership of studios by large corporations like Gulf+Western or TransAmerica, or to investigate how the wide impact of digital technology today has altered how movies are made and watched.
- The relationship of movies to their reception, demonstrated in an essay that explores how television in the 1950s changed the expectations of movie audiences at that time.

Although there are ways to write about film without emphasizing historical issues, some historical awareness informs most writing about film. An essay that examines *Mildred Pierce* (1945) in the context of post–World War II America and the changing sociological position of women would be based on a historical method, even though the direction and point of the argument may be a feminist critique. Similarly, an essay that presents a straightforward reading of the themes and style of *The Wild Bunch* (1969) could develop that reading by relating those subjects to the Vietnam War, the history of the western in American movies, or innovations in movie technology during the 1960s. Many exciting and informative historical essays have main topics that have little or nothing to do with the analysis of specific films and, instead, concentrate almost exclusively on historical facts and complexities—an economic crisis, say, or the political pressures behind an instance of censorship—that only indirectly figure in what an audience sees on the screen. When using a historical method to help explain a film, beware of assuming that any particular movie, even a documentary, gives an unmediated picture of a society and a historical period. To be sure, *Our Daily Bread* (1934) tells us a great deal about the early 1930s in America during the Great Depression, but what it tells us is bound up with historical questions concerning, for example, its style and intended audience. History is a delicate instrument; use it with as much discrimination as possible. In *Film History: Theory and Practice*, Robert Allen and Douglas Gomery note that "doing history requires judgment, not merely the transmission of facts" (iv). In this excerpt from their reading of F. W. Murnau's *Sunrise* (1927), they demonstrate how historical research can be used to fuel an initial curiosity about the lavish and artsy techniques of the movie:

William Fox's decision to hire F. W. Murnau and to give him virtually carte blanche in the production of *Sunrise* involved much more than the addition of one more "highly artistic picture" to the 1927–1928 Fox schedule. Fox used Murnau's considerable biographical legend as part of a carefully orchestrated plan to elevate the status of his studio to that of preeminence in the motion picture industry. In the mid-1920s, Fox occupied, along with First National and Warner Bros., a middle echelon within the film industry both in terms of economic power and product prestige. (Prestige can be defined as the extent to which the films of a studio are perceived to be of "quality" in the critical discourse of the period.) In the mid-1920s Fox was known as a producer of unpretentious, "folksy" pictures, not highly regarded by critics but for the most part popular with the mass audience. Examining the "Best Films" lists of *Film Daily Yearbook* and *Photoplay* for 1925, for example, we find that of 184 "best" pictures cited by 184 different critics, only 9 were Fox titles; in both lists the films of Paramount and MGM predominate.

In 1925, however, William Fox launched one of the greatest expansion plans in the history of the motion picture industry. The plan eventually collapsed with the stock market crash of 1929, but just before his downfall Fox controlled the production of Fox and MGM studios, Loews Theatres, Fox's own large theater chain, and a one-third interest in First National Theatres, British Gaumont, and assorted other holdings. The Fox drive for economic power in the late 1920s was paralleled by attempts to enhance the prestige of Fox productions, and it is in this context that Murnau's hiring and his production of *Sunrise* must be viewed. Fox anticipated that Murnau's production of the highly artistic picture would bolster his studio's "special" films category. Unless the specials could attract greater critical attention, Fox would never have the prestige to match his hoped-for economic status. (99)

If you decide that yours will be a historical approach, ask yourself specific questions about the role history will have in your argument: Is the historical information you use background or introductory information for your study? Are you concerned with how and why certain historical events are represented as they are in the movie? Does historical background help to explain narrative or technical maneuvers in the film? Does the movie stand out in history, or is it part of a historical trend? Is your argument intended to clarify that place in history? What is more important to your argument: the historical facts behind the film's production, how its successive audiences responded to it, or both? No matter what your specific subject, ask yourself what part history might play in it.

NATIONAL CINEMAS

If historical issues usually play some part in essays on the movies, another important (and related) way to discuss them is in terms of their cultural or national character. The presumption behind this approach is that film cultures evolve with a certain amount of individuality and that to understand, for instance, the complexities of Alexander Dovzhenko's *Arsenal* (1928), one must locate it first in the political and aesthetic climate of postrevolutionary Russia. Similarly, to analyze an Indian film of Satyajit Ray, such as *Distant Thunder* (1973), a writer should know something about the society and culture of India. According to this approach, ways of seeing the world and ways of portraying the world in the movies differ for each country and culture, and it is necessary to understand the cultural conditions that surround a movie if we are to understand what it is about. Because it employs many Western themes and formulas, an American spectator might have little trouble comprehending a film by Akira Kurosawa, but without guidance and some cultural background on Japanese society, the films of Kenji Mizoguchi or Mikio Naruse might seem too foreign and confusing for the average American student.

Observe how the author of the following passage identifies the specific cultural heritage of the African films of Ousmane Sembene and Med Hondo (Figure 4.01). While admitting the influences of other national cinemas (like the French New Wave of Jean-Luc Godard), he singles out an oral tradition that distinguishes and marks a range of different films as uniquely African:

Figure 4.01 Sembene's *Xala* (1974) reflects specifically African heritages and issues (concentrating, for instance, on communal more than on individual actions). Writing about this film thus always benefits from some familiarity with its national and cultural context.

Although African filmmakers invoke oral tradition as a primary influence, they have appropriated it and applied it in various ways to create paradigms for addressing the broad range of social, political, cultural and historical issues of Africa.… Although their styles are diametrically opposed to each other, this use of oral tradition and African film language can be identified in the films Ousmane Sembene and Med Hondo. While Sembene's narrative is more linear than Hondo's and imbued with straightforward didacticism (as in *Borrom Sarret, Mandabi*, "The Money Order," 1968, *Xala*, 1974, and *Camp de Thiaroye*, 1987), Hondo's films (*Soleil O*, 1969, and *West Indies*, 1979) are…syncopated and eruptive in tone, and reminiscent of the stylistically disruptive tone of black French liberationist literature. The two filmmakers not only share a number of Western influences (such as Italian Neo-Realism, Hollywood, Latin American documentary, and Soviet montage) but are indebted to indigenous oral storytelling techniques as well. Thus, while Western critics have tended to read Hondo's style as avant-garde and Godardian, Africanist discourse has emphasized its link with oral tradition. (Ukadike 571)

When deciding to discuss a movie or a group of movies from a foreign culture, a writer might begin by questioning, with an open mind, what exactly distinguishes these films from the American ones with which he or she is familiar. (This implies that, at the same time, the writer will sketch a sense of what is specific about the American cinema of a given period.) How do the meanings of these films change when they are seen outside their culture? In what ways might you, as an American, understand British films of the 1950s differently from the English audience at that time? What kind of cultural research might give you a better handle on the themes? Should you read something about the other arts, the politics, the economics of the movie industry there? Try not to oversimplify the connections between a culture and its films; remember that an approach of this kind implies (perhaps falsely) a unity or a fundamental similarity between many different films from a country. Could you find a similar kind of unity in American movies of the 1990s?

GENRES

A French word meaning "kind," *genre* is a category for classifying films in terms of common patterns of form and content. Many of us casually practice the categorizing behind genre studies when we view movies: Often, we identify a set of similar themes, characters, narrative structures, and camera techniques that link movies together as westerns, musicals, film noir, road movies, melodramas, or sci-fi films. Westerns feature cowboys and open, uncivilized spaces; sci-fi movies deal with adventures in outer space or intrusions by extraterrestrials. In analytical writing, a discussion of genre is frequently an effective way to begin examining how a film organizes its story and its audience's expectations. A western such as John Ford's *The Man Who Shot Liberty Valance* (1962) operates expressly out of a generic tradition, and although there may be many ways of talking about the film, one of the most important is to examine its subversion of many of the traditional patterns and expectations about the western. This particular movie is the tale of a western hero, but we discover that this hero is not like the usual western hero and are surprised by the intentional generic variation.

In the following passage, Vivian Sobchack discusses the genre of film noir. Rather than concentrate on well-known characteristics of this genre (such as stories of crime and the use of dark lighting), she highlights here the more subtle contrast between a house and home in this postwar genre:

> In [film] noir, a house is almost never a home. Indeed, the loss of home becomes a structuring absence in film noir. It is particularly telling to think here of the ironic "domesticity" that runs through *Double Indemnity* (1944) or *Mildred Pierce* (1945)—films that are linked irrevocably to noir but pose problems to its particular urban iconography. The suburban

house into which Phyllis Dietrichson invites insurance agent Walter Neff is merely a house: its furniture plain, its decorations sparse and impersonal, motel-like. It doesn't look lived in. Indeed, its interior decoration is best described in a line of dialogue offered by a character about a house in a later film noir, *The Big Heat* (1953): "Hey, I like this. Early nothing." And, even in her domestic beginnings, Mildred's home is also figured as merely a house: drab, plain, unmarked by the people who live there and supposedly constitute a family. The kitchen in which Mildred bakes her pies has none of the warmth and coziness of Norman Rockwell's kitchens and is hardly a felicitous space. And this lack of felicity is echoed in her voice-over narration that accompanies a flashback: "I was always in the kitchen. I felt as though I'd been born in a kitchen and lived there all my life except for the few hours it took to get married." (144)

In writing about a film genre, whether it's a romantic comedy or a horror film, always keep historical distinctions in mind, as Sobchack does here, because genres change with the times. Also identify for yourself what common structures, themes, and stylistic techniques are associated with a particular genre. When did this type of movie first appear? What are the antecedents outside film history—novels, opera? How has it changed through history, and why? Does the story of the movie you are analyzing fit the genre it seems to be placed in? If not, does the mixing and matching of generic formulas serve a purpose, as in *Blade Runner* (1982), in which the detective and sci-fi genres, among others, are superimposed? As genres mature through the years, you may discover a strange self-consciousness in a film's use of generic formulas, as in *The Man Who Shot Liberty Valance*. How is this self-consciousness used? Is it an attempt to poke fun at the genre, or is it an attempt to show the limits of the genre in describing the complexities of the modern world? Could *Little Miss Sunshine* (2006), a film about a dysfunctional family's journey to a beauty contest for young girls, be discussed as a madcap variation on the road movie? *Brokeback Mountain* (2005) is the story of secret sexual relationship between two cowboys; to what extent is its power and complexity a function of how the film consciously engages the tradition of the western and its masculine stereotypes?

AUTEURS

Auteur criticism is one of the most widely accepted and often unconsciously practiced film criticisms today: It identifies and examines a movie by associating it with a director or occasionally with another dominant figure, such as a star (say, Clint Eastwood). In a sense, referring to "a David Lean film" or "a Steven Spielberg movie" is in itself a critical act, because it implies that the unifying vision behind what you see on the screen is the director's and that there are certain common themes and stylistic traits that link films by the same filmmaker. Although writers refer casually to a dominant actor or even a screenwriter as an auteur (an "author"), auteur criticism has its historical roots in the claims of literary independence and creativity made by and for certain directors. Since the 1950s, it has become a standard strategy in writing about film, with the director understood to be the auteur who anchors and unifies our perception of the film. Here, Thomas Elsaesser examines characters in the films of Samuel Fuller and pinpoints general character traits and actions attributable to Fuller's guiding vision and consistent interests:

> One of the most distinctive features of a great number of Fuller heroes is their willingness—indeed their compulsion—to expose themselves to situations charged with contradiction. The Fuller heroes, as it were, come to life only under conditions of extreme physical or mental stress; they seem, and often are, on the verge of hysteria, and their mode of action betrays a kind of electric, highly explosive energy.
>
> Paradoxically, the impression one gets is that this apparent mental and emotional instability is what makes them strong in will and action. I am thinking of figures like the Baron of Arizona, Zack in *The Steel Helmet*, O'Meara in *Run of the Arrow*, Tolly Devlin in *Underworld USA*, and even Merrill in *Merrill's Marauders*. All live impossible situations, and knowing they cannot win, they nevertheless act with a kind of conviction, a kind of instinctive immediacy—as if they were engaged in an incessant flight forward, and were committing themselves to a course of action in whose perverseness they almost seem to rejoice, because they intuitively accept it as the fundamental condition of their existence. (291)

Although auteurism provides the foundation for many excellent studies, it should be used with some skepticism for at least two reasons. Rarely does a director have the total control that the term suggests, because anyone from a scriptwriter to an editor may be more responsible for the look and logic of a film. And what an auteur represents differs quite a bit depending on the time and place; *auteur* applied to French directors Truffaut or Eric Rohmer in the 1960s has quite a different meaning from *auteur* applied to Wes Anderson or David Lynch today. If you embark on a comparative study of the editing in two films by the same director, you should make it clear that you know you are using an auteur model and indicate how that tag applies to this director. Ask also how the historical conditions of film production encourage or discourage the auteurist unity you find in his or her work. Were the films made as part of a studio system, as were George Cukor's, in which the influence of the studio might be more noticeable than the influence of the director? Or did the filmmaker have a great deal of independence, as does the British filmmaker Peter Greenaway, and thus control over how the film looks? What are the most distinctive signs of the filmmaker's control over the film: Editing? The stories themselves? The themes? The setting? Are your expectations about a film conditioned by what you know about its director, as when you anticipate a great deal of violence from a Sam Peckinpah movie? Why? What kind of changes are there in the director's work over the years, and how do you account for them? Are there special marks of this filmmaker in each of the films, like Alfred Hitchcock's cameos, Josef von Sternberg's cinematic portraits of Marlene Dietrich, or Spike Lee's appearance as an actor in some of his movies? Keep in mind, finally, that sophisticated auteur studies are interested in the films, not in the psychology or private life of the filmmaker.

KINDS OF FORMALISM

Formalism is a name often given to film criticism concerned with matters of structure and style in a movie, or with how those features discussed in Chapter 3 (such as the narrative or the mise-en-scène) are organized in particular ways in a movie. In most instances, a writer will want to discuss these formal matters together with the major themes of a film, but the chief focus of a formalist essay will be on patterns such as narrative openings and closings, the significant repetition and variation of camera techniques, or the relation of shots and sequences to each other. In the context of a discussion of CinemaScope and by concentrating on color and space, the writer of the following excerpt presents an illuminating and exact account of a sequence in formalistic terms:

> In *Rebel Without a Cause* (Ray, 1955) a shot of extraordinary beauty comes after the first twenty minutes of the film, during which the surroundings have been uniformly cramped and depressing, the images physically cluttered-up and dominated by blacks and browns. Now, James Dean is about to set out for school; he looks out of the window. He recognizes a girl (Natalie Wood) walking past in the distance. Cut to the first day/exterior shot, the first bright one, the first "horizontal" one. A close shot of Natalie Wood, in a light-green cardigan, against a background of green bushes. As she walks the camera moves laterally with her. This makes a direct sensual impression which gives us an insight

into Dean's experience, while at the same time remaining completely natural and unforced. On the small screen, such an image could not conceivably have had a comparable weight. (Barr 10–11)

Strictly speaking, formalist criticism does not emphasize matters outside the film proper, such as the different effects a movie may have on audiences, the historical conditions of its production, or any other questions that are not immediately apparent on the screen. (Rarely today, however, do you find an essay that is purely formalist; usually a formalist analysis becomes part of other arguments about an auteur, film history, a genre, and so on.) A purely formalist analysis might therefore investigate narrative unity in *His Girl Friday* (1940), in which the two main characters propel the plot along through a series of confrontations and crises that begin in their divorce and end in their marriage. A writer may carefully look for stylistic or formal repetitions in the editing or lighting of a movie and may then describe how they work in relation to the rest of the film. Another option is to choose a visually complex scene or sequence and describe how it works and why it is important to the movie. Early in *Shane* (1953), for example, there is a quick and involved exchange of looks among Shane, the farmer, the wife, and the child, an exchange that sets up the social relationships for the remainder of the movie; a formal analysis could explain how the camera communicates so much so quickly. Whether you are examining a single shot or a pattern of images, ask yourself what is most interesting and significant about the formal features and how they add to the story and themes. Is it the mise-en-scène that appears most crafted or, rather, a series of camera angles? If you concentrate on a single scene or sequence, how do the sound, lighting, and camera movement interact to comment on or support the action of the story? How would you connect the formal features of the film with its themes?

IDEOLOGY

In one sense, *ideology* is a more subtle and expansive way of saying *politics,* at least if we think of politics as the ideas or beliefs on which we base our lives and our vision of the world. *Ideology* might refer to one person's belief in the sanctity of the family or another person's sense that civilization is basically progressive. When we see a movie such as *The Battleship Potemkin* (1925), *Hotel Rwanda* (2004), or *Client 9: The Rise and Fall of Eliot Spitzer* (2010), there is little chance of mistaking the different political messages at work in each. The first hails the force of a socialist revolution in Russia; the second describes the heroics of a hotel manager, Paul Rusesabagina, who saves over a thousand Tutsi refugees from the Hutu militia; and the third examines a possibly conspiratorial sex scandal that led to the resignation of the governor of New York in 2008. Less obvious, however, may be the messages about life and society communicated in films such as *The Sound of Music* (1965), *The English Patient* (1996), *The Departed* (2007), or *The Girl with the Dragon Tattoo* (2009). Like the majority of movies, these films present themselves as mainly entertainment, and their makers would probably resent any claim that there are unintended social or political perspectives at work here. Yet most of us would probably acknowledge that each of these has rather clear ideological messages about individualism, gender relations, the importance of family life, race, or European history. Similarly, many of us might see *The Godfather II* (1974) as an exciting and well-made gangster film, but a writer sensitive to the ideological values in the movie might see those elements as part of another perspective, one concerned with the business of capitalism:

> *Godfather II* clearly shows the destruction and/or unobtainability of the basic bourgeois values. They are not destroyed because they are inadequate per se; family ties, social mobility, quest for security, male companionship, and even religious values all relate and correspond to real universal human needs for community, love, respect, support, appreciation. Coppola demonstrates that the social institutions—nuclear family, Mafia family, ethnic community, and the Church—upon which the Corleones relied to provide and protect these values withered before the irrational, destructive forces of capitalism, the main goal of which is profit, not the meeting of human needs.
>
> Coppola builds up, interweaves, and finally destroys four levels of familial affiliations—the nuclear family, the Mafia family, the ethnic community, and the Catholic Church. Through careful juxtaposition, he shows how each strives unsuccessfully to create an ideal community. In all cases, the needs of business destroy whatever communal aspects these associations might provide. In fact, it is the very effort to conserve and support these families that becomes corrupted by business and destroys them. *Godfather II* works out on the level of human relations Marx's insight that capitalism, even at its best, must destroy human life and associations to exist. Thus, the more vigorously bourgeois society strives to achieve the ideals it has set for itself, the more destructive and corrupt it becomes. And this contradiction is most clearly visible in American gangsterdom, the perfect microcosm of American capitalism. (Hess 11)

In critical writing attuned to ideology, any cultural product or creation carries, implicitly or explicitly, ideas about how the world is or should be seen and how men and women should see each other in it: The clothes you wear express social values just as the films you watch communicate social values. Whether we agree or disagree with the values expressed in a particular movie, the ideological critic maintains that these movies are never innocent visions of the world and that the social and personal values that seem so natural in them need to be analyzed. Good writing of this kind usually avoids the obvious politics of propaganda in a movie like *The Green Berets* (1968), in which the American presence in Vietnam is naively hailed, and instead looks into the more subtle and less definitive politics of a film like Mira Nair's *Mississippi Masala* (1991), in which the filmmaker tells a complex story of interracial romance in the American South.

The following six approaches are the principal ideological schools of film criticism today. Each attends not only to the films themselves, but also to the ways those movies are made and understood by audiences:

- Studies of Hollywood hegemony focus on how classical film formulas dominate and sometimes distort ways of seeing the world.
- Feminist studies investigate how women have been both negatively and positively represented through the movies, often with special attention to the history of women filmmakers that begins with the pioneering work of Alice Guy Blaché at the beginning of the twentieth century and continues through contemporary directors, such as Marleen Gorris or Su Friedrich.
- Race studies concentrate on the depiction of different races in films, such as Latinos, African Americans, and Asian Americans.
- Class studies analyze the social and economic arrangements shown in a movie to illustrate how social power is distributed in and through certain films.
- Postcolonial studies examine movies within a global perspective, aiming to reveal the repression of or emergence of indigenous perspectives within formerly marginalized or colonized cultures (like India or Iran).
- Queer theory investigates how normative relations can be challenged or disrupted through films, especially through confrontations with heterosexual values.

The best examples of ideological criticism attempt to avoid limiting themselves to the content of a movie; instead, sophisticated ideological criticism relates questions about characters and plot to more complex points about the shape of the narrative or the distance of the camera from the characters: What, for instance, is the ideological point of a war movie in which the enemy is seen only in large groups or in which the camera makes them all look alike? (In this kind of analysis, the intentions or claims of the filmmaker should not necessarily be accepted as what the movie is truly about.)

With an ideological approach, begin by trying to pinpoint what message or messages a film aims to communicate about its world and, by implication, our world. What is it saying explicitly? What is it saying implicitly? What does the film suggest about how people relate or should relate to one another? Is individuality important? Is the family important? Is the film straightforward and direct about those values and what they demand, both gains and losses? Are these values depicted as "natural," and, if so, why? Does the movie challenge the beliefs of its audience, or support them? Why? How do the politics of the film and the way it entertains intertwine? Particularly with issues related to gender and race, ideological criticism today offers many exciting ways to look at movies: how movies depict women or minorities, how movies exclude people of color, and how movies are seen by audiences outside the middle class. Above all, ideological approaches urge you to be suspicious of what you might normally take for granted.

As you read and write more about film, you will encounter other approaches to writing about film to add to the list of principal approaches

Figure 4.02 For a perceptive and flexible writer, Oscar winner *Slumdog Millionaire* (2008) responds to numerous critical perspectives and approaches. Aside from a formal analysis of its sounds and images, it can be investigated as a genre film that shares characteristics of Bollywood musicals, as an auteur film with themes found in other films by director Danny Boyle, and even as a film with complicated ideological issues about class and gender.

described in this chapter. And you will find that these approaches overlap and can be used with various degrees of emphasis, depending on what you wish to say about the movie. Writing about a film by Krzysztof Kieslowski (such as the 1993 *Blue*) would probably involve the writer in questions about Kieslowski's status as an auteur, his place in both Polish and French cinema, and both the historical and the formal features of his films (a short or even medium-length paper is not likely to allow this much scope). You should consequently never be too restricted by a particular approach, nor should you hesitate to work out other ways to write about film. Yet knowing these models and being conscious of when you may be using them can be extremely valuable in organizing your thoughts and in bringing your writing into focus. Most important, recognizing different ways of looking at the movies and writing about them will enable you to choose which method or methods best suit your own interests and aims (Figure 4.02).

SAMPLE ESSAYS

This first essay, written by a knowledgeable film student, examines Fritz Lang's *M* (1931) primarily as part of a tradition of German cinema and within the larger context of German culture and politics of the early 1930s (Figures 4.03 and 4.04). Observe, however, how formalistic questions and auteurist assumptions also play a role. In the second essay, a student who began only with an uneasy feeling about a film's portrayal of women demonstrates an ideological approach to *Ordinary People* (1980). More precisely, her essay is a feminist reading of the movie: It is less concerned with what the film intends to say than with what it does say about how women appear in a male-dominated society. Note that this "reading against the grain" of the film nonetheless remains very close to the images and actual story.

M. Trillo

The Reflection of *M*: Germany as a Culture of Crisis

The title is a specific and accurate description of the paper's content. The opening is general but engaging.

Fritz Lang's 1931 *M* is a suspenseful and horrifying tale of a psychotic child murderer. Its technical accomplishments alone make it worthy of attention: an economic and imaginative use of sound, sophisticated crosscutting editing, and graphic compositions which are sometimes as detailed and evocative as paintings. Because of these accomplishments, *M* will probably

Figure 4.03 The normal man on the street becomes a menacing reflection of himself in Fritz Lang's *M* (1931).

always appeal to audiences of different generations and from many different countries. But for my purposes, Lang's film is most intriguing as a reflection of a turbulent German society in the early 1930s. Whether consciously made in this way or not, *M* seems to work as a mirror image of the rise of fascism in Germany, but in reflecting that rise, the film may be most important as an attempt to expose it to the German audience that was so involved in fascism and its growth.

A question or problem is stated—which leads to a clearly announced and focused thesis.

German culture in the 1920s and early 1930s was, as is well known, caught in a crisis. The gradual collapse of the Weimar Republic from 1919 to 1933 created a society that seemed to live in a kind of chaos

A brief but pertinent discussion of cultural and historical background.

T.S

Figure 4.04 The mirror images of *M*.

or disorder, a chaos that was economic, social, and psychological. Poverty, unemployment, and depression became widespread realities, and the stable sense of a personal identity once found in a German tradition and a very ordered society seems to have been destroyed by the catastrophic defeat of World War I. This general disorder and instability are reflected in many of the major cultural trends of the period. The nightmarish dream paintings of Norwegian Edvard Munch are

The background material is related more specifically to artistic traditions.

the very influential emblems of a whole school of German expressionist artists whose focus was on the dark, turbulent world beneath the quiet surfaces of everyday life. Freud's writings also became more and more important during this period. This increasing importance is especially appropriate since his work discusses the dark unconscious below men's and women's conscious life and also sketches a civilization full of secret discontents (Willet).

The source for much of this information is cited.

pulls info From Source & summ

Kracauer and Lotte Eisner have shown, some of the most important movies made during this time depict a "haunted screen" reflecting much of the unstable reality of the society. From *The Cabinet of Dr. Caligari* to *Nosferatu, the Vampire*, many of these films seem regularly to be about madness and destruction, and even in the realistic "street films," the settings and plots describe a world that is collapsing into ruin. In the tyrants and madmen that often control the chaos in these movies, many viewers have seen the foreshadowing of Hitler, the Caligari who would step in to use the insecurity of the crisis as a vehicle for massive destruction (Kracauer, Eisner).

The cultural and historical context is further focused on two key film movements, highlighted with references to particular films and two scholarly sources. Throughout this paragraph, the writer reminds his readers of the original title and thesis ("the crisis"). Likewise, it becomes a useful transition word in the topic sentence.

T.S brings in films from time period same & same style

These motifs are central to *M*, which draws from that expressionist tradition in which Lang himself worked during the 1920s. The central character Beckert (Peter Lorre) is a man possessed by something he cannot control, a mad compulsion to murder children. Beneath his placid and calm exterior and in the midst of everyday life, the insane killer begins to throw the world into disorder. Stylistically, the film draws on both the expressionist and the "street realism" traditions of German film. The insanity is

T.S

The German expressionist cinema of the 1920s was likewise concerned with this crisis and its depiction. The first sentence works as both a transition ("these") and a topic sentence, pointing to the analysis of the single film in question. Very short summary of the film's central theme.

Still focused on the film, the writer connects formal and stylistic questions to the larger culture and social history. "Conversely" connects discussion of two German film traditions that inform the movie.

shown, on the one hand, in a number of expressionistic shots, like the spiraling staircases that indicate entrapment and a dizzying lack of perspective. Conversely, there is the street realism of social poverty and underworld life which gives *M* a kind of documentary look at times. Unlike in some expressionist films, it should be noted, it is difficult to distinguish in *M* between the dream world of psychological chaos and the social chaos of the street. Or to put it in terms of the story, Lang makes it difficult in this postexpressionist movie to say whether Beckert is an evil madman or a victim of some force that runs through the whole society.

Topic sentence reasserts central thesis and introduces analysis. Specific, concrete examples are described, along with the precise technical detail from the film. A personal reflection is inserted—one that intelligently expands the themes of the film.

The movie makes this confusion and the crisis it implies fairly explicit at times. The balloon, which becomes the symbol of one of Beckert's victims, has a pudgy human shape, and its resemblance to Beckert's shape might suggest a connection between the killer and the victim. The law and order of the police who search for Beckert are, through Lang's parallel crosscutting, identified with and almost indistinguishable from the underworld crime mob that searches for Beckert, too. Lastly, there are the carefully orchestrated mob scenes (as during the final trial), which nonetheless appear as hysterical and bloodthirsty as the pathetic murderer seems. (In these instances, I can't help but think of the murderous actions of the Nazis in the name of law and order or of the perfectly ordered crowds of soldiers who became the machines of war.)

A transition and summary ("There are, then"), which then moves to the central point of the essay: mirror images.

There are, then, a number of double images or double reflections in *M* that seem to muddle the questions about a society in crisis. Where does the

More concrete description that attends both to what is seen and how it is formally presented.

crisis originate? Where is the order, and where is the disorder? What is the nightmarish dream, and what is the reality? This double image and the questions

T.S.?

it provokes are most apparent in the character of Beckert, specifically in the number of times that he and the audience are made to examine his image. Frequently, Beckert examines himself and sees himself in mirrors, searching out the madman that exists somewhere inside him. At one point, Lang shows Beckert looking in a shop window, where the image of Beckert is contained in a frame within the film image—a frame made by a reflection of knives laid out in a diamond shape inside the store. Here, the normal man-on-the-street becomes a menacing reflection of himself. Later, Beckert discovers he has been found out and exposed by seeing a reflection in another mirror image that reveals the telltale "M" on his back.

What the reflections expose in these different shots and scenes is not exactly the same thing. Yet, in each, it is the dark side, the disorder, the murderous impulses of self (and society) that are sought out and

T. s a general more specifics come back to T.S.

The writer expands his analysis of certain themes and formal strategies (the crisis contained in the "mirror images") to describe how the images on the screen address and challenge the audience.

discovered. In most of these mirror images, furthermore, the camera places the audience at an angle so that it seems to *participate in that reflection—looking either over Beckert's shoulder or* directly into the reflection itself. Just as the film builds up a strange sympathy for the madman Beckert, these mirror images seem to force an audience to view its own darker side in the reflecting images of a psychotic killer.

Some further summary that condenses (but doesn't repeat) the argument.

If *M* is, then, like other German films of the late 1920s and early 1930s, an indirect reflection of a German culture in crisis, it is also more than a simple reflection.

A dramatic broadening of the main points of the essay, but this time in terms of the history of the filmmaker, the auteur behind the film.

Combining the two traditions of expressionism and street realism, it makes nightmares real and reality a nightmare in a manner far more disturbing than most other German movies of the time. Perhaps this is what the German authorities recognized when they forced Lang to change the original title, *A Murderer Among Us,* because they thought it was too politically provocative. When Lang fled Nazi Germany a few years later, he probably realized, however, that no movie, even one as powerful as *M,* would be enough to stop the tyrannical darkness that was surfacing in the streets of Germany.

Works Cited

Eisner, Lotte. *The Haunted Screen.* Berkeley: Univ. of
      California Press, 1969. Print.

Kracauer, Siegfried. *From Caligari to Hitler.* Princeton:
      Princeton UP, 1947. Print.

Willet, John. *Expressionism.* New York: McGraw-Hill, 1970.
      Print.

A title that succinctly but explicitly indicates an argument or engagement with the main theme of the movie. The opening paragraph introduces a common understanding about what the film means, then moves quickly to state the writer's alternative "point of view." Concentrated in the final sentence, the thesis and argument are focused further by being related specifically to the main character, Conrad.

The Not-So-Ordinary Women of *Ordinary People*

   Ordinary People is intelligently acted, well scripted, and critically and financially successful. It is apparently an "honest" look at upper-middle-class America, presented as an impartial record of one family's emotional turmoil and ultimate collapse. Yet, seen from another perspective, this supposedly honest and impartial movie can be viewed as a careful construction of women as agents of disaster or failure. When examined from this point of view, the women in *Ordinary People* are consistently seen and shown from a male perspective in which they function mainly to devastate and disrupt the already shaky state of the film's protagonist, Conrad Jarrett.

Thesis

The topic sentence recalls the thesis but shifts its emphasis to the centrality of male relationships and the isolation of women.

Male bonding pervades this movie but is always overshadowed by the threat of invidious females, especially the chilling character of the mother, Beth. The force of this threat is particularly evident during the daily rituals of eating, that domestic sphere traditionally controlled and orchestrated by women exiled to the kitchen. Around and within these eating rituals, we best

The negative characterization of the mother is dramatized specifically in terms of her actions in the kitchen—a dramatic, visual space that allows the writer to integrate details of the editing, the dialogue, and the composition of the images.

see *the subtle violence* and manipulation on the part of the mother. Early in the film, for example, Conrad struggles to return to "normal" life after his suicide attempt and subsequent stay in a mental hospital. A casual call from his father to come to breakfast panics Conrad, and a swift sequence of shots interweaves his distress and the mother's efficient, machinelike preparation of food. By the time he enters the kitchen, looking ill and nervous, we are his visual comrades, flinching along with him at the painful tension within the break-fast ritual: While the dialogue remains superficially ordinary, the quick editing between faces and actions makes it clear that breakfast with this mother is anx-iously violent. When his mother serves him French toast and tells him it is his favorite, he quietly says he is not hungry, and without a word, she whisks the plate away before a close-up shows her viciously stuffing it down the garbage disposal. The father and son can only react with bewilderment to this unpredictable female, who in this early scene is already established as less balanced than the skittish son.

When it is obvious that the family breakfast has been destroyed by the mother, the father, Calvin, tries to save the situation by suggesting that Conrad bring his male friends home to "play touch football on the

More concrete detail, important to support an argument that critiques the "intended" meaning of the film. Note that incidents from the film are used not simply to recount what happened but to support an idea and an interpretation.

A strong transition is made from the previous paragraphs with the phrase "asserts itself again."

Technical and stylistic evidence, described precisely.

The writer continues to alternate the two key points in her argument about "male bonding" and female disruption. At the same time, she depicts this as a "developing" problem that the film's narrative will work to solve.

lawn." His attempt to rescue one ritual with another is more exactly an attempt to replace female trouble with male bonding. Calvin invokes a whole team of males to replace the shattered scene resulting from the mother's punitive violence. At this point in *Ordinary People,* however, her presence is far too strong, and the reunion of the father and the son must be delayed through a full series of narrative encounters and revelations.

The mother's presence asserts itself again shortly after the breakfast scene, this time in a dinner scene vividly underlined by the stylistics of the film. The scene opens with a medium-long shot that gradually tracks in through a dining-room doorway. The shot is rigidly balanced as the frame of the doorway lines up perfectly with the sides of the film frame, and the dining-room table is in the gradually opening center of the frame. The mother is at one side of the table, Conrad at the other, and the father in the center. Within this balanced frame and the commonplace conversation, Conrad seems safe. The mother begins, though, to press him about his "torn shirt," and he immediately shrinks from her gaze. When he answers another demanding question by saying he hasn't played tennis in a long time, Beth snaps back, "Well, don't you think it's time you started?" appearing unusually threatening and tall as the camera holds on her from a low angle for a noticeably long time. In the background of the shot is the father, looking small and uncomfortable; the rapid cutting and close-ups emphasize that the original balance of the scene was merely delaying the fragmentation it at first disguised.

More concrete detail, important to support an argument that critiques the "intended" meaning of the film. Note that incidents from the film are used not simply to recount what happened but to support an idea and an interpretation.

Calvin again attempts to bond with his son in the wake of the mother's aggressive attack (which is exactly how this "ordinary" moment is portrayed). He asks Conrad the name of his female friend from the hospital, a person who the audience knows is important to Conrad. Beth then immediately announces her implicit control of the scene by leaving the table as if to abandon the distasteful topic (and probably the competition of another female). From that point on, she is physically absent from the table yet very much in control as she oversees the two males from the back of the shot. Knowing this, they exchange silent but meaningful glances, the only real communication the camera has so far allowed them while under the tyrannical eyes of the mother.

A major expansion of the argument claims that the crisis the mother represents is part of a much larger problem with women in the film.

These examples do not, it must be emphasized, describe simply a tale about one bad woman and mother. All the females in *Ordinary People* are inept; all women fail Conrad. His meeting with Karen, the friend from the hospital, is, despite its promise, especially disappointing. She carefully denies the friendship they formed at the hospital by concentrating the conversation (appropriately in a restaurant) on her new appearance of normality and her adjustment to an "ordinary" world. A school play is much more important than any intimacy she and Conrad may have shared in the hospital: "That was the hospital; this is the real world." She exudes a cheerfulness and enthusiasm that Conrad's troubled spirit cannot match, and in many ways, she seems to be becoming a replica of Conrad's mother, interested only in appearances and unable to respond to male "substance."

The theme of normality and the ordinary returns.

The argument about the problem with women is expanded through the significance of Conrad's girlfriend, who represents "weakness" in the name of propriety.

Even the most redemptive female character, his newly found girlfriend, Jeannine, ultimately abandons him. Again at a restaurant, she tentatively reaches out to him by asking him about his suicide attempt. He responds by saying she is "the first person to ask" such a question, and he begins to answer her in what appears to be the first therapeutic act of communication in the movie. Just then, they are interrupted by a rowdy group of males (mostly the athletes who describe another theme in the film); she reacts by giggling and allowing them to pull her from the table, thus destroying the potential bond between her and Conrad, who is visibly shaken by the incident. In the logic of this scene, she is clearly the one who has failed Conrad after he opens up to her, and later, she tries to explain it by saying she laughed out of embarrassment at being singled out by a group of males. In effect, she, like the other females in the movie, sacrifices Conrad to a so-called feminine sense of propriety.

Sharp transition from the weakness and propriety of the female characters to the need for the male characters to separate themselves from that world to be reborn in male camaraderie. The first part of the paper described the suppression of that bonding; this section describes how that bonding can be rediscovered through the rejection of women. Phrases of dialogue are inserted into the writer's sentences to make the point.

In *Ordinary People*, this sense of propriety becomes aligned with a feminine weakness that is seen best in the subplot of the father's rebirth as a man. In his conversation with a business partner (both jogging athletes), he regrets his inability to fire incompetent female secretaries who "crack gum in your face." And when he turns to Conrad's psychiatrist while looking for a way to deal with his wife's coldness, he comes away from this new male bond realizing how weak his wife has made him by dominating him with her femininity. (She made him change his shirt the day of their son's funeral because it didn't look right.) The father discovers that he needs to be strong, that he no longer loves his wife because she may be "beautiful" and "unpredictable" but is "not strong, not giving." Conrad discovers, through the same psychiatrist and his confrontation with the "weak" suicide of Karen, that he has superior strength, which is why he survived the boating accident. That strength is what finally allows the men to banish the weak and destructive mother, and with her departure, they are free to bond in a male embrace.

A concise summary of the argument crystallizes the point in a single scene and shot.

Ordinary people are therefore men who are strong but do not know it and women who fail those men by not allowing them to bond as men. In the ordinary style of this movie, the two-shot of men communicating becomes the longed-for goal of the movie (attained at the conclusion), and in one of the most revealing scenes in the movie, when the father prepares to take a snapshot, a two-shot, of mother and son, the mother refuses to participate. The point is obvious, even if unintentional: If an intimate two-shot with a male is the test of an honest reality, in *Ordinary People* women are clearly excluded from it and the reality it represents.

point

illustrating in a new way in conclusion

Exercises

1. Identify the approach or method that seems most appropriate for a specific film. Write three or four paragraphs that discuss that film according to that method.

2. Select a single film to discuss from the angles of two different methods. Devote two paragraphs to each method and show how each offers different perspectives on that film.

5

STYLE AND STRUCTURE IN WRITING

Perhaps the greatest temptation and the most common danger in writing about film is to approach your material as if you are simply "at the movies." Describing and analyzing what you have seen as if it is only the subject of a casual conversation or a "sneak preview" for your friend or classmate will not, finally, result in an effective and polished piece of writing. Good writing about any topic is improved by a relaxed style, but the lure of film's immediacy should not distract you from the care and preparation that a film essay requires. The following guidelines sketch many of the fundamental steps and tools underlying good writing. If they are obvious, let them act simply as reminders.

In *Day for Night* (1973), director François Truffaut comments on the inevitable gap between the grand conception of a film and the nuts-and-bolts execution of that plan. Writing about film is similar. In both, the final expression of our ideas involves adjustments and work that, as Truffaut suggests about his movie, may change and even improve that original conception. This means, above all else, that the tools for executing those ideas—in this case, the principles of effective writing—must be attended to with the same care that the writer took to conceive of those ideas. We have all seen movies that are based on a brilliant idea but fall flat because of poor technique. Writers should be wary of a similar mistake.

When a viewer watches and reflects on a movie using the various approaches and critical vocabulary discussed in the previous chapters, the actual writing of an essay can be considerably easier. Some of the usual anxiety about finding ideas and arguments should be relieved if one methodically follows those steps.

If you have taken good notes, you have gone a long way in the "prewriting" stage. The next most crucial element of the essay is a clearly focused topic—a *thesis*—that will allow you to get at the film or films from a workable angle. This clear focus will also allow you to do a thorough analysis in a limited number of pages and, at the same time, expand the topic along broad-enough lines to keep your reader interested. Even if your instructor presents you with a general topic, you will usually have to refocus it so that it is more specific and personal. Discussing racism in D. W. Griffith's *The Birth of a Nation* (1915) could prove too large a topic for a ten-page paper. Conversely, an essay focused on a truly minor detail, like the furniture used for one set in that movie, could prove too trivial for a long essay unless handled with dexterity and developed through research.

The scope and focus of your essay will depend, as we have noted, on the audience you foresee for it. An informed audience will not be interested in a familiar plot or such information as "Griffith was an American filmmaker." The sooner a writer determines the audience, the sooner the parameters of the essay will start to take shape. This is a critical step in writing about film, because much of what you say and see, particularly during a second screening, will be guided by those parameters.

Another central task of the first stage of writing is *outlining* your topic. Many skillful writers do not work with an outline, finding it too constricting. Others find outlining absolutely necessary, especially because of the fleeting nature of a film. Under the best circumstance, a writer sketches out an outline while organizing notes into a coherent point of view on the film. An outline can take any form, ranging from clusters of observations and thoughts to a series of main points to a formally numbered and sectioned blueprint of an argument, complete with headings and subheadings. Outlines can provide real assistance with the logic of an argument. An outline that is clearly thought out can be invaluable when you are viewing a movie for a second or third time. It becomes a kind of viewfinder that enables you to spot significant details missed on the first screening. Here, in one student's brief outline for a paper on Todd Haynes's *I'm Not There* (2007), the writer uses full sentences to make certain that complete ideas will define the main sections of the argument (Figure 5.01):

Sharon Conway

I'm Not There and the Invention of Identity

I. While Todd Haynes's film about the life of Bob Dylan, *I'm Not There*, might at first glance appear to be a typical "biopic," its striking use of six different actors to represent Dylan is only the most dramatic indication of a more complex and wide-ranging investigation of human identity and how identities are constantly being reshaped and reinvented.

Figure 5.01 Writing an essay about a film as complex as *I'm Not There* (2007) will always benefit from a plan that clearly outlines the logic of the essay.

II. Biopics are a common and traditional film genre focused usually on a famous individual from history.

   a. Traditional biopics rely on narrative coherency and continuity to represent its subject

   b. Two examples of traditional music biopics: *The Glenn Miller Story* (1953) and *The Doors* (1991)

III. Dylan's life appears as a series of contradictions and unpredictable changes

   a. From life as a hobo to Christianity

   b. Dylan's identities through his songs

IV. Rather than disguise the contradictions and changes in Dylan's life, *I'm Not There* celebrates them as a testimony to the flexibility, creativity, and inventiveness of the individual identity.

   a. How six different actors create different Dylan identities

b. How identity is always a performance in the largest sense

c. How the fragmentary narrative structure and dramatic cinematographic style reinforce that dynamic of invention as the key to modern identities

V. Conclusion: The title of Haynes' film thus contains a slightly ironic key to the film: while, for many, the elusive Dylan may not be "there" because he seems to change roles and identities so often, the absence of a permanent, singular self is exactly what, for Haynes, makes Dylan a model for the many creative ways we can change and grow.

When the paper is written, it will probably depart from this outline and will certainly become more defined and more specific. Yet, an outline of any kind can be the foundation on which you build more complex ideas.

THE RIGHT WORDS

Concrete Language

The actual writing of the essay involves guidelines that are basic to all writing and are important to rehearse and recall frequently. Because a film critic is recreating a film and a perspective on it through language, sensitive and accurate use of words is paramount. Concreteness is the heart of some of the best film writing, largely because the reader depends so much on the visualization of a scene or sequence. Also, the accuracy with which a writer describes what he or she sees is often the most convincing way to make a point. After seeing a striking sequence from Werner Herzog's *Fata Morgana* (1971), an inexperienced writer might be tempted to write, "There was a series of strange shots, with crazy dialogue and odd characters." An experienced writer, like the author of the following passage, revitalizes the images with a lively and concrete idiom to comment on them:

> The strongest sequence may be a catastrophic metaphor of hell on earth: a catatonic drummer and a tacky female pianist on a tiny stage in a brothel perform a piece they have played a thousand times without any emotion, endlessly, off-key. "In the Golden Age, man and wife live in harmony," the commentator says, as they are photographed head-on, with all the merciful cruelty of a humanist filmmaker who must show

everything. At the end of the piece, they remain immobile. There is no applause. (Vogel 76)

Denotation and Connotation

Denotations and connotations are other rhetorical tools that can be used effectively or ineffectively by a writer. A *denotation* is the dictionary meaning of a word; thus *film* and *movie* have the same denotation. If you mean *sequence,* don't say *shot;* if you mean *Hollywood style,* don't be satisfied with *classical style,* because the latter term could indicate a specific kind of Hollywood or European movie. Be precise: Say what you mean and avoid words that have little denotative value, like *thing* and *aspect.*

A *connotation* is any association or implication of the word you use. *Film* has for many people sophisticated, intellectual connotations, while *movie* has connotations associated with mass entertainment. Both *Hollywood* and *classical* carry a number of connotations (*commercial* or *establishment,* for instance) that a writer should be aware of when using them. Mack Sennett, the founder of the Keystone Kops, warned against inappropriate critical language when he said there "was a wonder and a miracle" in his films which "no amount of expensive grammar can explain."

Tone

The tone of an essay can vary considerably, from the jaunty sarcasm of some newspaper reviewers, to the pretentious didacticism of some film theoreticians. *Tone* is the total effect of the words you use and how you use them, and every essay establishes a tone, or "writer's voice." Be conscious of the tone of voice you are adopting in your argument; some tones are less appropriate than others. Sarcasm, humor, and anger are among the least effective tones to use in formulating an engaging and convincing argument. A paper that begins, "This so-called art film could never appeal to a normal audience," immediately identifies the writer as someone too prejudiced to make balanced judgments. The same point can be made with a more balanced tone: "The problem with art films is that they may alienate a public used to a more accessible story." A writer needs to find the right compromise between a casual voice and a formal one. The nature of that compromise will depend on you and the specific topic of your essay. Too much slang won't work, nor will pretentious words that you normally don't use. A writer conscious of tone will maintain a consistent one throughout the essay, not changing tone of voice from sentence to sentence or paragraph to paragraph.

Finally, beware of using quotation marks around words to try to create an indirect or clever tone or sarcasm. If you mean that a character behaves like a dominant and oppressive male stereotype, don't be satisfied by simply writing that he is "a 'really liberated' guy." Quotation marks used in this way rarely explain anything. They usually blur what you mean.

Repetitions and Clichés

A common difficulty in word usage is to keep the diction fresh and varied. Experienced writers rely on the *repetition* of key words for emphasis and continuity. But the lazy or uncontrolled repetition of words results in tedious prose: Repeated references to "the director" throughout a short passage can be irritating. You can easily correct such repetition by substituting a proper name (*Romero*) or an article (*he*). When you find yourself locked into unnecessary repetitions, vary your descriptions and phrases, but don't force a change by using terms that do not fit your style.

The tendency to depend on *clichés* is a version of the same problem: the substitution of a quick and unexamined use of language for precise expression. The snatches of jingles and pat quips that we often find in movie reviews are an extreme version of this use of clichés. They indicate how meaningless terms like *blockbuster* or *a film everyone should see* become.

In the following passage, Robin Wood employs several phrases we have all heard before ("very much in question" or "a great pity that"), and he builds his point around the repetition of words like *energy, ridiculous, artist*, and *violence*. Here, however, Wood demonstrates how common expressions can contribute to a relaxed tone and how the repetition of a word sometimes leads to finer distinctions in thought:

> The value of Sam Peckinpah's work is still very much in question; its intensity is not. And art that expresses such energy and passion, such commitment to personal impulse, commands, at least, respectful attention. *The Wild Bunch* (1969) and *Straw Dogs* (1971), whatever one's estimate of them, have that combination of candor and force which announces an artist who is not afraid of appearing ridiculous; those who profess to find them no more than ridiculous are perhaps nervously insulating themselves from the films' ferocious and contagious energy. At the same time, one may comment at the outset that it is a great pity that, in the eyes of the public and most critics, Peckinpah's gentler and arguably finest films...have been so overshadowed by the spectacular and explosive violence of the more notorious works—a violence that is certainly a major component of his artistic personality, but by no means the whole story. (771–72)

EFFECTIVE SENTENCES

Economy

A writer should aim at two key stylistic goals: to be economical and to be interesting. Being economical means saying precisely all that you need to say and cutting words and expressions that add no information or serve no stylistic purpose.

Many writers get stuck for words and are not able to come up with sentences that adequately express a thought. When this happens, going back to an outline and talking through your ideas in terms of specific images and sequences will help start the flow of sentences. The inverse problem, however, is equally troublesome: Sometimes a writer who spews out words in haphazard fashion loses the meaning of his or her sentence in the process. A critical eye notices that the following sentence is unnecessarily wordy:

> There are many difficult and demanding scenes in this film by Lina Wertmüller, *Swept Away* (1975), which give the movie an operatic quality.

Cutting and economizing, the writer would revise it to the following:

> Lina Wertmüller's *Swept Away* (1975) is a demanding, operatic film.

You can usually eliminate wordiness of this kind by watching out for redundancies, wordy constructions (for example, "there is"), correctable uses of the passive voice ("Edgar Wright directed *Scott Pilgrim vs. the World* [2010]," instead of "*Scott Pilgrim vs. the World* [2010] was directed by Edgar Wright"), or merely words that could be deleted without changing the sense of a sentence. Reviewing the following passage, the writer should have recognized its extreme wordiness:

> Despite its central and obviously important role in the way a movie communicates, one of the most overlooked and ignored areas of study in film scholarship is proving to be the many variations and appreciable differences in how movie dialogue has been used and how its functions have changed rapidly through history and dramatically from director to director.

Without sacrificing information, the better, more succinct version reads as follows:

> Despite the central role of film dialogue, most scholarship has overlooked its evolution in films and its various uses by different directors.

Varied Sentence Structures

An interesting style requires more than just an interesting subject to write about. It also requires a way of presenting the subject in sentences that dovetail and emphasize your material in the strongest way possible, because holding a reader's interest—always a goal of any writer—requires sentences that present your analysis in its most effective form. Some authors "shoot from the hip," naturally and chattily presenting their points in lively prose. Most of us, however, tend to get stuck in stylistic ruts, of which the most common in student writing is the unvaried use of simple declarative sentences. To escape these ruts, we use several stylistic strategies to make our sentences more flexible and emphatic.

Parallels draw attention to the relations between or the equation of two or more facts or ideas:

Hollywood movies have three purposes: to entertain, to make money, and to advertise a way of life. [Do not write "to entertain, to make money, and advertising a way of life."]

Coordination joins two related sentences with a conjunction (*and, but, or,* and so on), the result being a compound sentence and a rhythmic variation in your sentence patterns:

Hollywood movies are meant primarily to entertain and to make money, and less obviously, they aim to advertise a way of life.

Subordination combines two or more points or sentences into a single complex sentence that redistributes those ideas to deemphasize some points and emphasize others:

Although Hollywood movies aim to entertain and to advertise a way of life, their primary function is to make money.

In the following sentences, the writer has gotten stuck in sentence structures, and the writing is choppy and tiresome:

Ingmar Bergman is the premier Swedish filmmaker. He has been active in film and theater since 1944. His most famous movie is probably *The Seventh Seal* (1957), and this film dramatizes typical Bergman concerns with theological and social angst. His most visually complicated film is *Persona* (1966), and it examines that angst as it relates specifically to images, personalities, and the cinema.

Revising these sentences, the writer communicates the material far more effectively and economically through parallels, coordination, and subordination:

Active in film and theater since 1944, Ingmar Bergman is the premier Swedish filmmaker. Although *The Seventh Seal* (1957) is his most famous movie, his most visually complicated is *Persona;* while the first dramatizes typical Bergman concerns with theological and social angst, the second examines that angst as it relates to images, personalities, and the cinema.

In making these sentences a bit more economical, the writer has also made them more emphatic: in the first sentence, by subordinating less important information about Bergman's past; in the second, by creating parallel phrases that compare the two films and by subordinating the less interesting *Seventh Seal.* The original sentences could have been restructured in many ways. Their structure should be determined not only by economy but also by what the writer wishes to emphasize.

When you are composing your first draft from notes and reflections, it is probably best not to labor over finding the exact word or the most economical phrase. At that stage, your objective is to get your ideas down on paper as quickly and as completely as you can. The time for correcting and polishing sentences is usually when you revise that draft, when you should be more sensitive to how you can improve your writing.

COHERENT PARAGRAPHS

In a movie, the elements that compose the mise-en-scène (actors, props, and so on) become part of a shot; many shots develop into a scene and then a sequence, and sequences can be combined to form a narrative. The growth of an essay can be conceptualized according to a similar scheme. Perhaps writing is never quite so schematic, yet, just as an accurate and resourceful use of words leads to lively sentences, well-constructed sentences become unified and coherent paragraphs.

There is no set length for a good paragraph nor is there an absolutely correct number of paragraphs for a given paper. A five-hundred-word essay normally has four or five paragraphs, and a developed paragraph usually contains at least four or five sentences. However, the number of paragraphs and their respective lengths will depend on the ideas in your argument. Ideally, the number of paragraphs in an essay follows from a thorough and well-conceived outline. If you have only two or three paragraphs or very short paragraphs, your argument may be short on good ideas, or those ideas may not have been thought out fully or supported concretely. (Although journalistic writing, such as a newspaper review, frequently relies on very short paragraphs, this is usually *not* the kind of paragraphing appropriate for a critical essay.)

Whether the paragraph has a few sentences or a dozen, it must contain an idea that clearly unites its sentences. This unifying idea should be made explicit in the *topic sentence* of each paragraph, a sentence that pinpoints the guiding concept of the paragraph. When you locate this sentence at the beginning of a paragraph, you help the reader to follow the train of thought throughout the paragraph. Sometimes your topic sentence will be the second sentence. Very rarely is a topic sentence unnecessary, and in most cases, you should not use, in place of a topic sentence, a *plot sentence* that simply retells some of the plot. Generally, a topic sentence anchors the paragraph and announces its central idea, even if that idea is then developed through two or three other related ideas. Note in the following paragraph that the central idea ("the repose of the Western hero") is clearly identified in the first sentence. Note also how the author creates a smooth transition (from the previous paragraph about the gangster film) through the appropriately placed "by contrast":

> The Western hero, by contrast, is a figure of repose. He resembles the gangster in being lonely and to some degree melancholy. But his melancholy comes from the "simple" recognition that life is unavoidably serious, not from the disproportions of his own temperament. And his loneliness is organic, not imposed on him by his situation but belonging to him intimately and testifying to his completeness. The gangster must reject others violently or draw them violently to him. The Westerner is not thus compelled to seek love; he is prepared to accept it, perhaps, but he never asks of it more than it can give, and we see him constantly in situations where love is at best an irrelevance. If there is a woman he loves, she is usually unable to understand his motives; and he finds it impossible to explain to her that there is no point in being "against" these things: they belong to his world. (Warshow 137)

Here, characteristics of the Western hero are described separately: his perspective on life, his breed of loneliness, his feelings about love and violence. Each, however, can be referred to and is subordinate to the central topic of his "repose." Like most good paragraphs, this one features a general and clear beginning and then moves through specific points to a strong and emphatic conclusion.

The next example of paragraphing has a more complicated structure. Note its successful use of transitions ("In more general terms," "yet," "however," and so on) to connect parts of sentences, separate sentences, and separate paragraphs:

> In terms of sound quality, the average film of the mid-forties, whether in Hollywood, France, or England, represented a significant improvement on the original efforts of the late twenties. In more general terms,

however, the films of the forties remained the direct descendants of those earlier films. Every step of the process had been improved—from microphones to printers, from amplifiers to loudspeakers—yet the fundamental optical recording and printing technology remained basically the same. Not until after the war, thanks in part to German wartime technology, did the sound recording industry in general and the film sound track in particular take a quantum leap forward with the perfection of magnetic recording techniques. As with all important technological developments, however, the magnetic recording revolution met with immediate economic resistance. There was no question that magnetic recording was easier, used lighter, more mobile equipment, cost less, and produced decidedly better results; theaters, however, were not equipped to play films which substituted a magnetic strip for the traditional optical sound track. Just as Hollywood delayed the coming of sound for years, it has for economic reasons delayed the coming of better sound for decades. Over a quarter of a century after the general availability of magnetic recording technology very few theaters (usually only the high priced, first run, big city variety) are equipped with magnetic sound equipment. Ironically, for years, the average amateur filmmaker working with super-sound equipment has possessed better and more advanced sound reproduction facilities than the neighborhood cinema.

Nevertheless, Hollywood was able to capitalize on the new technology in another way. Though filmmakers around the world continued to use optical sound for distribution prints, they very early began to do all their own recording in the magnetic mode (by the end of 1971, 75 percent of Hollywood's original production recording, music scoring, and dubbing was being done on magnetic recording equipment). Finishing what the playback had begun, magnetic recording divorced the sound track still further from the image and from the image's optical technology. Now, any number of sound sources could easily be separately recorded, mixed, and remixed independently of the image (thus simplifying the manipulation of stereophonic sound now often coupled with the new wide-screen formats). (Altman 48)

These are rather complicated paragraphs, in part because a great deal of information is proffered and in part because more than one idea is at work in the first paragraph. Specifically, the writer is discussing two ideas like a kind of two-sided coin: On one side, there are the advances made in sound technology in the post–World War II period (announced in the opening sentence); on the other side, there is the failure of Hollywood to implement those advances.

The author balances and contrasts these two developments by mapping the logic of their progression from the prewar period to modern times, and he connects them through key transition words like *however*. Notice also how this back-and-forth progression is deftly focused in the middle of the first paragraph with the sentence beginning "There was no question"; this sentence has a parallel structure, its two halves divided by the semicolon and each side representing a version of the twofold point the paragraph is making. Also, the coherence and vividness of the paragraph are enhanced by numerous concrete details and historical facts. (When you are writing papers more analytical than historical, this kind of information may not be as necessary, available, or appropriate, but always attempt to solidify and flesh out the idea of your topic sentence with hard facts or concrete details from the film.)

Finally, the passage demonstrates a neat transition between the two paragraphs that turns on the word *nevertheless* and the phrase "in another way." Make sure your transitions between sentences and between paragraphs add clarity, coherence, and fluidity to your essay. Using words or phrases specifically suited for this purpose, like *furthermore* or *in fact*, is one way to increase coherence; a second method is repeating key words from the end of the previous paragraph, as this writer does with *Hollywood* and *technology*. Always make sure that your reader can follow a logical transition from one paragraph to the next.

INTRODUCTORY PARAGRAPHS

Many of us—like Alvy Singer, who in *Annie Hall* (1977) refuses to enter a movie even a few minutes late—know how important a beginning is. Although many Hollywood films settle quickly into mediocre stories and styles, the first ten minutes can provide the most captivating and innovative sequence of the entire experience (which is a way of keeping you in your seat). Beginnings are crucial to any presentation, and no matter how long your essay will be, getting that first paragraph right could be the most important revision of your essay.

An essay must hold a reader's interest if it is to communicate information or make a point, and the introductory paragraph is where that interest should first be piqued. Starting your paper with a string of commonplaces—that Frank Capra was an American director, that his films were very popular, and so on—is not likely to encourage your reader to continue reading. Even when a reader (say, your instructor) is obliged to finish reading an essay with a dull beginning, that first paragraph creates an expectation about your work. The first paragraph is the ideal place to give your reader a clear sense of what your topic is and how you intend to develop it: the *thesis statement* that tells exactly and specifically what is the argument of the essay. Even in long and ambitious essays, that direction is clearly announced as a signpost and provocation for the reader:

> In the late 1930s, public discussion about Hollywood changed. Clergymen in backwater towns could still raise a crowd by railing against sin on the silver screen, and judges and reformers here and there continued to maintain that movies led impressionable youth to crime. Among academics and in literary circles, however, and in the principal newspapers and magazines, the moviemakers were regarded with considerably more respect, awe and even envy, as the possessors of the power to create the nation's myths and dreams. (Sklar 195)

The essay's title, "The Making of Cultural Myths: Walt Disney and Frank Capra," catches the attention of many readers who recognize both names but would not necessarily place them on common ground. As with all good openings, however, the introductory paragraph does not simply restate that title ("This essay will discuss cultural myth in the movies of Walt Disney and Frank Capra"). Instead, it introduces its topic in terms that are more general and, at the same time, more concrete. Starting with a specific historical reference (the late 1930s), the paragraph describes a specific historical transition in the debate between those who thought the movies were frivolous and those who believed they were an important cultural medium. With that debate as a background, the paragraph moves to its thesis about the power of the movies of Disney and Capra to create social myths.

NOTE: Whether you formulate a title before you begin writing this first paragraph or after you have finished a final draft, always make the title an informative and enticing entry into your first paragraph: It should be broad enough to suggest the scope of your topic but specific enough to get your reader interested. "Cultural Myths" would have been far too general a title for the previous example; "Walt Disney and Frank Capra" would have been too quirky and unclear.

An opening paragraph should identify the object of study (here, moviemakers of the late 1930s) and the topic the writer is focusing on (here, history and cultural myths). Often, the focus is the analysis of a particular film or part of a film. You can organize a first paragraph by moving from a general proposition to a specific statement of your argument. Or, as the last example shows, you can move from specific examples to a more general (but not too general) thesis that your paper will develop.

Introducing a provocative quotation or a specific image is one way to energize a first paragraph. Whatever method you use, your aim is to convince your reader immediately that you have something worthwhile to say, an argument that needs airing, observations that are not readily apparent. Although the rest of your paper will develop and expand on these first propositions, you should make very clear here what your essay is about and what method you will use to investigate your topic. If you compose and focus this paragraph to fit the length and limits of your paper, that paper will be much easier to write: Nothing is more common and more disastrous than the massive thesis statement ("This is a study of *Black Swan* [2010]") formulated when a writer doubts he or she can find enough to say about a more narrowly focused topic.

In many ways, the first paragraph is the most difficult of the essay; it presumes you know pretty much where the argument is going, although some conclusions are often arrived at in the writing itself. Although it is important to formulate an introductory paragraph in the first draft, you should plan to reexamine and rewrite that paragraph in a later draft. At that point, an effective first paragraph will become much easier to write.

CONCLUDING PARAGRAPHS

For some students, a popular strategy for reaching a conclusion is to rephrase the opening thesis in slightly different words ("Thus, I have shown..."). This approach, however, frequently seems mechanical and dull. A concluding paragraph, like an opening paragraph, is best when it makes your reader attend to it and to sit up and realize that something interesting has been said that may have implications beyond the bounds of the essay. Some summary is not necessarily a bad idea, especially when an argument has been a bit complicated or involved; even so, earlier ideas should be retrieved not merely to remind the reader of what has been said, but to emphasize a final, often more expansive, point, as Tom Gunning does in this conclusion to his discussion of the 1902 *Trip to the Moon:*

> Perhaps most important, as I stated at the opening of this essay, *A Trip to the Moon* endures not as a fossil of a forgotten early history of the cinema, but as a film whose energy and imagination, visual design and sense of humor, technological innovation and sense of wonder still delight audiences today. Perhaps more than any other early film, it embodies the high spirits that marked early cinema, the excitement of discovery and innovation that marked the new medium. Méliès's tongue was lodged firmly in his cheek as he presented his fairy-tale vision of the future, in which scientists still dress as wizards and the inhabitants of the moon perform acrobatic stunts. But he also expressed the human

desire to reach the moon, to walk the surface of the earth's satellite, to find wonders where no one had gone before. (78-79)

As Gunning's conclusion demonstrates, conclusions should not attempt to wrap up a complex argument too neatly and sweeping generalizations are risky. Some of the most effective conclusions close an argument within the range of that particular essay, at the same time opening it to other questions.

In concluding a discussion of Leni Riefenstahl's films and photographic work, Richard Meran Barsam moves carefully from the specific to the general, referring to historical figures and titles, arriving at some definite conclusions about the woman and her work yet maintaining a relatively balanced and open-minded tone that points the reader toward other questions:

> The Nuba film will be similar to her other work because it will express again the special world that has engaged her imagination since she was a child. Leni Riefenstahl's world is a world apart, a world of crystal grottoes, of men who think they are supermen, of the human body made godlike through film, of elite warriors on a dark and foreign plain. This world exists in fact, but it becomes in her imagination a very different entity. Protected by her belief in that entity, which is, of course, her art, Leni Riefenstahl remains apart from much of the everyday world. She cannot understand why many people in that world will not accept her or her legends; as she publishes her Nuba photographs (to some, a bold and striking act of penance), she thinks that these documents will show her belief in man's honesty, goodness, and oneness with nature. The Nuba photographs do show those aspects, of course, but they are photographs of a disappearing world. Fortunately for all mankind, her photographs of Hitler represent another world that has disappeared, but the world will not forget that she found it necessary, and perhaps even advantageous, to make those pictures and to create the myths that infuse *Triumph of the Will* with its terrifying power. A truly enigmatic woman, Leni Riefenstahl fights against the legend that she has created for herself, fights against it even as it encloses the final years of her life. Leni Riefenstahl is one with her legend, inseparable from the world that she has made. She has what every artist since Daedalus has dreamed of, except the power to fall, to admit error, and to transcend the fragile barrier that stands between art and life. (37)

For some, the final rhetorical flourish here might seem a bit much. Conclusions and openings are always more rhetorical than other paragraphs, however, and whether or not they choose a more matter-of-fact tone, writers should strive to get as much out of their words as possible—especially at the crucial points in an essay.

REVISIONS AND PROOFREADING

One common and dangerous writing error is to presume that once a good draft of the paper has been finished, the most important work has been done. Although revisions of that essay may seem simply, for some, like polishing the finished material, good writers know that one of the most important steps in writing is to move carefully through one or more detailed revisions, followed by a focused proofreading of each line. No one writes a perfect draft the first time, and most good writers go through several drafts before they feel comfortable and secure with an essay. If you grow weary, remind yourself: Film scripts may be subjected to a dozen rewrites before a director starts to film, and once the film is made, its editing may become another series of revisions. The time you allow between your first draft and your revision should permit you to look at the essay with fresh eyes. Check your logic, topic sentences, and thesis statement (does it still fit the paper you wrote?). Check to see that you argue and develop your thesis rather than merely assert it. Be prepared to change, delete, and add both small and large parts of the essay in order to improve its argument and style. Reading through the essay, watch for awkward expressions, poor transitions between sentences and paragraphs, and imprecise words. Are your examples still relevant? Are your quotations accurate? If you have time, put the paper aside again and then do one last revision. Finally, proofreading means rereading the essay with fresh eyes, watching for overlooked mistakes in spelling, punctuation, or grammar. If these seem like minor details, remember that, with writing as with many films, the importance of appearance should never be underestimated.

CHECKLIST FOR WRITING AN EFFECTIVE ESSAY

Each writer has personal methods and strategies. The following are some summary guidelines, suggestions, and reminders:

1. Be prepared for a movie. Before you see a film, ask preliminary questions about when and where it was made and about your own expectations concerning it. Ask which of your other interests—technology, art, business—might point you in a good direction when writing about film.

2. Learn to look carefully at the movie and to take notes. Let your general, preliminary questions become more specific and concrete as you respond to the movie. What seems most important in it? What seems most unusual about it?

3. Let your questions lead you to a manageable topic that involves both the themes of the film and its technical and formal features. A topic like "The Search for Identity in *Citizen Kane*" is probably too large for a short essay; a much more compelling topic would be "Kane's Childhood: The Beginning of an Identity Crisis." The more concentrated focus of the second topic will allow you to examine scenes and sequences in detail.

4. Try to view the movie at least one more time after you have decided on a topic. Expand your notes at this point, filling in details you may have missed during your first screening.

5. Keep clarifying your argument; transfer your notes to a computer file (or note cards or a notebook if you prefer). Begin your argument with a statement of the problem or question you intend to address. Then assemble and lay out the specific points of your discussion, using concrete evidence from the movie and your interpretation of it. Good essays usually proceed from less debatable thematic points to more complex points about style and technique. Remember, you are presuming that the reader has seen the movie but will need to be convinced of the point you wish to make.

6. Many writers find it useful to sketch out the organization of an essay in outline form. Depending on your habits and preferences, your outline may be very complete and detailed or rather general and sketchy. If you tend to have trouble with organization and paragraphing, you will want to make it as complete as possible. For each section of the outline, you may even wish to write full sentences as headings; these may later become your topic sentences.

7. Begin to write. For many professionals as well as students, this is the most difficult part, and we all have too many ways to put it off (taking more notes, watching the movie again, checking your email, and so on). Delays do not make the task any easier. Creating an outline can help because it consists of actual writing, but when it does not help enough, you should write down your ideas freely or randomly. Step back and imagine explaining your topic to a friend. Aim merely to get some sentences written; you can re-sort and refine your ideas later.

8. As you write, keep thinking about your subject, pushing your ideas further. Most of us don't know exactly what we think about a complex subject until we start to articulate our thoughts. Writing itself becomes a discovery process of which we should take full advantage. Check your logic by sketching an outline of what you have written. Polish your first paragraph and conclusion. Consider some larger questions about your approach. Is it mainly historical or formalistic? Are you interested in the cultural identity of the film? If you are emphasizing a particular method, decide to what extent your approach should be acknowledged early in your paper.

9. Regularly save and back up all your writing on your computer.

10. Revise; always revise. Allow as much time as possible between your first draft and your revision of it, preferably a few days. Follow your final revisions with a careful proofreading to catch any minor mistakes or typographical errors. NOTE: It can be very useful to revise at least one draft on a hard copy—even if you intend to submit an electronic copy of the essay—rather than revising directly on the computer, since errors are easier to spot when the writing is in hard copy.

11. Print out a clean copy, following the guidelines about margins, footnotes, and so on (see pp. 155–162). Be certain you are not breaking or bending any rules about plagiarism (see pp. 160–163).

Exercises

1. Outline an argument for an essay using headings and subheadings for each section. Use full topic sentences for the headings.

2. Write three different versions of an introductory paragraph so that the thesis becomes more and more specific with each version.

6

RESEARCHING
THE MOVIES

Research improves any piece of writing. Normally, few people see a film or begin to write an essay about it with all the facts or a record of other opinions before them. When you exchange opinions with a friend, exhaustive background information may not be necessary or even relevant. Yet as soon as you have a point to make or an argument to present, as soon as you have a stake in what you are saying, then the more you know about the subject and the issues related to it, the more satisfying it will be to write about it.

Two equally intelligent friends may watch Paul Schrader's *Mishima: A Life in Four Chapters* (1985), and although each may have perfectly sensitive and sensible responses to it, the one who has knowledge of Japanese culture or the facts of writer and filmmaker Yukio Mishima's life will have a richer and more detailed reading of the movie and be able to support her or his evaluation better (Figure 6.01). Although both may understand the themes and recognize that the elaborate structure and style are central ingredients in their reaction to these themes, the viewer who can connect them to other Schrader films, such as *American Gigolo* (1980), *Affliction* (1997), or *The Walker* (2007), will be able to detect variations and complexities in motifs concerning obsessiveness and alienation that escape the less knowledgeable viewer. If that person also takes the time to read Schrader's book *Transcendental Style in Film,* some of Mishima's literary work, and something about Schrader's problems with the widow of the celebrated Japanese writer, that person could offer information and insights about the movie that would distinguish his or her essay from "just another opinion." A well-researched argument, one that brings to bear facts and observations outside the ken of the average viewer, is often all that distinguishes the authority and sophistication of one perspective from the impressions of another.

You can use research in a number of different ways. It can be integrated into your essay to support your own points with the authority of other writers, or it can be used to introduce a common perception against which you wish to argue. Notice how this writer, Paul Julian Smith, skillfully orchestrates and streamlines considerable background research

Figure 6.01 *Mishima* and Paul Schrader: researching the man and the filmmaker.

on Spanish filmmaker Julio Medem as a way of beginning his discussion of the film *Chaotic Ana* (2007):

> It is no surprise, then, that film scholars have been drawn to this rare example of auteur cinema. In his 2007 book on the director..., Rob Stone has celebrated Medem's work as a continuing intimate narrative which he claims is based on uniquely personal references and aesthetics. Nuria Triana-Toribio has offered a more critical account in *Spanish National Cinema...*, suggesting that scholars have seized on Medem as an artist whose supposed purity of vision "redeems the commercial sins" of Spanish cinema, defending its honor at home and abroad. One recent Spanish volume on Medem, which combines critical essays and extensive interviews with the director, is called *Contra le certeza* (*Against Certainty...*). The title suggests, paradoxically perhaps, that it is Medem's uncertainty—his ideological skepticism and his refusal clearly to direct his audience—that provides the constant guiding thread that any auteur's *oeuvre* must exhibit. (30)

Many of us might have trouble summarizing so many scholarly sources in a short introduction, and sometimes a single provocative quotation is enough to locate your own point of view. Yet, however and wherever you use research, it can quickly substantiate and direct your writing if you use it wisely.

Writers of film essays are traditionally divided into two camps that are distinguished by their different approaches to research; one group is made up of critics and reviewers, the other of scholars and historians. Those in the first camp interpret a film through their own analysis and feelings about the value of the movie, and researching material other than what is on the screen is usually considered unnecessary. The scholar-historians, however, are concerned mostly with that other material: the history of the movie's production, critical responses to it, theoretical suppositions, and facts or information that are not at hand when they go to the movies. For the scholar-historians, understanding a movie involves a significant amount of research into the ideas and historical background that have determined what appears on the screen. For the critic or reviewer, Orson Welles's *The Magnificent Ambersons* (1942) speaks for itself; the power of the story and the style of the movie would be the focus of the discussion. For the historian, however, Welles's battles with the studio and his inability to complete the editing on his own terms become the most important part of the analysis.

Some writers emphasize either scholarship or a personal critical response, but most writers operate somewhere in between. Competent reviewers for a newspaper or a magazine usually bring a fair amount of prior knowledge (about film history, the director, or the background of a particular film) to bear on their discussion of a movie. Likewise, good scholar-historians do not just accumulate "dry facts" or cover theoretical issues that have little to do with why we like or dislike a film. Their investigations are based on a desire to throw more light on what certain movies mean or why we value them.

Research involves anything from checking a date to examining the entire economic history of a film. Whether your topic is an interpretation of an individual movie or a description of the technology behind it, good research should shape your feelings about how the film can be understood and enjoyed. Research is not simply accumulated facts or ornamentation; a good writer always *engages* research, making clear, for instance, why it is important to her argument, where she agrees or disagrees with other positions, and how she intends to use it. As a prelude to a discussion of the "vanishing woman" in four Bette Davis films, the writer of the following paragraph uses historical research on Davis's other films, as well as research on print material related to Davis's outspoken career, as part of a clearly stated engagement with that material and rationale for her argument:

> Rather than examine a common example of Gloria Swanson as the vanishing woman of *Sunset Boulevard* (1950), I have taken Bette Davis as an alternative figure for this inquiry for a number of reasons. First and perhaps most importantly, Davis literalizes the star's endless cycle of vanishing and reappearing by playing a fading star no less than four times within the course of her career: in *Dangerous* (Alfred E. Green, 1935) for which she won an academy award; *All about Eve* (Joseph Mankiewicz, 1950); *The Star* (Stuart Heisler, 1952); and *Whatever Happened to Baby Jane?* (Robert Aldrich, 1962)....Davis was no stranger to the real possibility of professional disappearance. In September 1962, soon after the completion of *Baby Jane*, she placed an ad in the Hollywood trade papers, stating: "Mother of three—10, 11, and 15—divorcee, American. Thirty years' experience as an actress in motion pictures. Mobile still and more affable than rumor would have it. Wants steady employment in Hollywood."...The starlight of Bette Davis repeatedly illuminates the ambivalent space of vanishing and return, a space in which both vision and visibility and are strained and unstable. (Beckman 161–62)

HOW TO BEGIN RESEARCH

How much and what kind of research a writer does depends on variables such as the time available and the length of the project. Having three months to write a twenty-page paper will presume and require more research than a five-page essay due in two weeks. A review written in two days normally contains only the research that the writer has immediately available or that is found in press notes; a scholarly essay will involve research done over many months.

The quality and amount of research material available depend on the film and when it was released. A writer who begins work on a classic film, such as Victor Fleming's *Gone with the Wind* (1939) or Marcel Carné's *Children of Paradise* (1945), finds more essays and books than can be satisfactorily examined in a reasonable time. Conversely, in the months immediately after its release, even a highly publicized Hollywood film, such as *The Da Vinci Code* (2006) or *Burlesque* (2010), usually has generated only newspaper and magazine reviews and interviews, and a writer choosing to write on a recent foreign movie or an unheralded Third World film might have trouble locating even one or two short reviews. The usefulness of these materials is extremely different: A dozen superficial reviews of a film or a coffee-table book on a director may offer little more than variations on plot summaries or gossip, while a small, intelligent review or one exceptional book could provide you an entire foundation or backdrop for your own ideas. Research is a learned skill, and the good writer develops methods of quickly finding what is available and efficiently sorting out what is most pertinent to his or her essay.

Each person develops an individual research technique. Some people prefer to read background material before seeing a movie. Some work better when they think through their position on a film and then investigate how that position contrasts with or complements the existing body of opinion. Many writers' habits fall somewhere between these extremes.

Even before seeing the movie, try to get a sense of it by considering preliminary questions (for example, when it was made and its intended audience; see Chapter 2). After seeing the movie, clarify what you think about it and what interests you most. (Writing about something you find uninteresting can be the most difficult kind of writing.) Once you have sketched your ideas about a movie and then focused those ideas on one or two topics, you have the parameters within which to direct your research. This kind of preliminary focus is particularly important when your topic has generated a great deal of critical literature through the years, because it allows you to distinguish what research is relevant to your argument and what is not. The student who intends to write on a Hitchcock film, for instance, can easily be intimidated by the large number of books and critical essays about that director. When the student focuses the research on "the use of sound in Hitchcock's *Psycho*," the task immediately becomes more manageable. Keep in mind that although some subjects may prove too large for a paper, very few are too small if you think carefully about them. The most important guide is your own interest.

Research should be done with an open and discriminating mind. A good writer is willing to be redirected down new paths and, if necessary, to change a position. The student researching Hitchcock and sound may, on reading other writers, decide instead to work on the music alone or to do more research into Hitchcock's's collaborations with Bernard Herrmann to discover how they affected the sound in his later films. The writer disappointed with the comparatively little serious work on a period in film history, such as that of Nazi Germany or in non-Western cultures, must be ready to explore topics outside film history itself by reading some more general cultural or political histories. Research both develops and tests a writer's ideas. Adjusting or changing ideas is part of the excitement of doing research.

The trick is to learn to recognize what is important to your essay and what is not, what to keep and what to discard. The process is made easier only when you are, at the same time, prepared with ideas and flexible about changing them. Indeed, René Clair's description of filmmaking in "How Films Are Made" suggests a similar process for researching and writing about film: "The idea for a film is sometimes born in an author's mind, but more often a film company has the intention of making a film and is thus moved to search among existing ideas for the one that suits it best" (226).

When you have researched a subject and reworked your original idea, it is advisable to see the movie again. With a sharpened sense of what you want to say, you will invariably discover new information and find previously missed images that support your ideas. Just as your research is influenced by your first ideas after seeing the movie, your sense of what you wish to say is sharpened by seeing the film again. The inverse of Godard's pronouncement quoted at the beginning of Chapter 2 is thus, "Said better, seen better."

THE MATERIALS OF RESEARCH

Research materials have conventionally been divided into primary sources and secondary sources. Primary sources are the films themselves and the material directly involved in the films. Secondary sources are the books, essays, and reviews you read about the movie. Thus, a person wishing to write on the movies of George Roy Hill would go first to the primary sources: the movies themselves, a recording of the sound track, and even the script, if available. After consulting the primary sources, the writer may investigate secondary sources, such as a review, a film history, or a book about Hill.

Primary Sources

In film research, even gaining access to a primary source may pose some difficulties. Traditionally, researching a movie has been inhibited by the real obstacle of not being able to see the movie exactly when and as often as you would like. If your subject is a mainstream movie that happens to be playing at a local theater, this difficulty is relieved somewhat because you can see the movie several times—at least for as long as your financial resources hold out. Frequently, though, the films that interest you are not in regular distribution, and special strategies are required to supplement a first screening.

DVDs and Digital Downloads A seasoned researcher often uses archives or special arrangements with distributors to view authoritative versions of movies that have been damaged or cut through the years. Students, who usually have neither access to nor need of these facilities, must discover easier ways to view the films they are studying. Today, DVDs and digital downloads (through Netflix, iTunes, Amazon Unbox, or other "video-on-demand" Internet services) substitute for or supplement the films themselves. These forms of film, however, must be viewed with caution and skepticism for several reasons. Many films, from *The Ten Commandments* (1956) to *Beowulf* (2007), rely on a wide-screen image (or, in the case of the latter, the gigantic IMAX image), so that even in letterbox formats for television screens, the image is dramatically different from its original. Finally, home viewing conditions create a kind of response to a movie very different from that to a theatrical screening. Viewers may have very different experiences of Griffith's *Intolerance* (1916), Hitchcock's *Vertigo* (1958), Kubrick's *2001: A Space Odyssey* (1968), or James Cameron's *Avatar* (2009) if they watch one of these films on a movie screen and then on a video monitor or iPod.

DVDs, cable or satellite movies, and digital downloads are, however, now the most common media for watching films, and it would be a mistake to deny their value for film research. With more and more films aimed at television showings and with an increasing number of directors crossing back and forth between film and television, the aesthetic and commercial line between the two is becoming less distinct. In fact, some movies we see at a theater these days seem to have been made for the television screen. More important, the widespread availability of different viewing technologies and the resurrection of foreign and forgotten films on disc or cable make these tools an almost indispensable aid to film research. A writer should make every attempt to see a film first on a movie screen, but the advantage of being able to analyze that movie further on disc or as a download is considerable. A student can study a single sequence or even a single frame in detail; other films by a director or from the same historical period can be compared. More esoteric movies are becoming more available through video stores than through film distributors.

Additionally, many DVD releases contain "supplementary features" such as deleted scenes, behind-the-scenes documentaries, audio commentary tracks by the filmmakers, interviews with the cast and crew, storyboards and production stills, filmographies, and even critical essays. Many of these features often provide valuable insight regarding the creative decisions made by the filmmakers and the technical processes involved in making a movie. Often, DVD releases of films are available in extended versions (sometimes called a "director's cut") or "unrated" versions and will therefore differ from the version originally shown in the theater. These "special edition" DVDs can be found for mainstream Hollywood movies (distributed by Universal, Warner Brothers, and so on), B-level genre movies (distributed by such companies as Anchor Bay Entertainment), and also foreign or "art" films (for example, through the Criterion Collection or Kino International). Some good online sources for purchasing or renting DVDs include the following:

> The Criterion Collection (http://www.criterion.com). DVD distributor of the well-known masterpieces of international art cinema, Hollywood classics, and often-overlooked gems from film history.
> Facets Multimedia (http://www.facets.org). Nonprofit organization providing online DVD rentals and sales.
> Kino International: The Best in World Cinema (http://www.kino.com). DVD distributor of many of the most important films throughout film history and around the world.
> Netflix (http://www.netflix.com). Online DVD rentals and streaming movies.
> Scarecrow Video (http://www.scarecrow.com). Largest video store on the West Coast, providing online DVD rentals and sales.

In addition to these sites, others offer free access to clips and occasionally entire films. Usually the films available are limited and rarely include contemporary fare:

> Hulu (http://www.hulu.com). Features clips and episodes from popular movies and television shows.
> Ubuweb (http://www.ubu.com). Allows users to download rare documents from literary, film, video, and music history, such as a Dadaist magazine from 1917 or a documentary on Andy Warhol.

YouTube (http://youtube.com). A continually evolving collection that ranges from personal videos to classic films; a good source especially for older films.

Movieclips (http://movieclips.com). Blogs, clips, and videos that allow users to compare scenes or sequences by the same director or with the same actor.

Metacafe (http://metacafe). A site that offers clips from and commentaries on sports and television shows and movies and music.

Scripts Published scripts are a primary source for studying a film. Film scripts have become increasingly available from traditional publishers and from online sources, but the kind of information they offer varies a great deal. A writer researching a film whose script has been published may find merely dialogue. Sometimes he or she may also find camera directions and detailed shot reproductions. Sometimes a published script may even contain interviews and essays about the movie. Keep in mind that published screenplays of films may differ significantly from the "shooting script" and from the film itself; never base an analysis totally on a published screenplay.

Secondary Sources: Books, Indexes, Journals, and Electronic Sources

Film books abound; you should begin your research into secondary sources by checking the resources in your library for what is available on your subject. Look under "Movies," "Film," "Cinema," and "Motion Pictures," as well as under headings that deal more specifically with your subject matter. If your topic concerns horror movies of the 1930s, for example, check for relevant titles under the four main headings and then look for titles under "Horror Films" or "The Supernatural." You could also check the headings for those national cinemas that relate to your subject (e.g., "Mexican Cinema"). While researching individual titles, it is efficient and practical to write down bibliographical information—author, full title, publisher, publication place and date, and page numbers—on note cards, even if you do not use all those titles.

In addition to a library's own collection, students are encouraged to take advantage of the growing number of other electronic database systems when researching a topic. Many of the widely available systems, such as Academic Index, LexisNexis, or ComIndex, incorporate research on film and cinema studies. More traditional research sources, such as the *MLA International Bibliography* or *Magill's Survey of Cinema*, can also be found on electronic databases. Always check with your research librarian to find out which database systems available in your library contain material pertinent to your work. Accessing these from a single computer screen is often an extremely efficient means of doing research.

Once you have gathered the appropriate books, you have the task of culling the information you need from what is a sometimes large pile. One quick way to get started is scanning the preface or cover to see if the book deals with the material usefully. In addition, look through the table of contents to see if the chapter titles point in the direction of your own thinking. When your topic concerns one or more specific movies, consult the index of the book to see how frequently and fully your films are discussed. Some books on horror films may be irrelevant "picture books"; others may be detailed histories that will become helpful only after you have a better understanding of your topic. To separate the books that offer either too little or too much information from those that seem to address your subject and films most appropriately, select one or two of those that seem most manageable to serve as introductory texts. If they prove satisfactory and helpful, use their bibliographies to guide you to other sources.

Besides the specialized books on film that can be found in a library, there are guides, encyclopedias, and film dictionaries that provide quick access to dates and historical information about a movie, a director, or a film movement. Although these rarely offer analysis of or argument about a film, they give solid factual information and introductory commentaries. Of the many available, here is a sampling:

The American Film Institute Catalogue of Motion Pictures Produced in the United States: Feature Films, 1911–1970. 5 vols. Berkeley: University of California Press, 1989–97.

Ascher, Steven, et al. *The Filmmaker's Handbook: A Comprehensive Guide for the Digital Age.* New York: Plume, 1999.

Baskin, Ellen. *Enser's Filmed Books and Plays: A List of Books and Plays from Which Films Have Been Made, 1928–2001.* Aldershot, England: Ashgate, 2003.

Bawden, Liz-Anne, ed. *The Oxford Companion to Film.* New York: Oxford University Press, 1976.

Blandford, Steve, et al., eds. *The Film Studies Dictionary.* New York: Oxford University Press, 2001.

Cowie, Peter, ed. *Variety International Film Guide.* Los Angeles: Silman James Press, 1964–. Annual.

Dyja, Eddie, ed. *BFI Film and Television Handbook.* London: BFI, 2001–. Annual.

Elsaesser, Thomas, ed. *The BFI Companion to German Cinema.* London: BFI, 2000.

Film Daily Year Book of Motion Pictures. New York: Film Daily
    Publishers, 1918–. Annual.
Halliwell, Leslie, and John Walker, eds. *Halliwell's Who's Who in the
    Movies.* 15th ed. New York: HarperCollins, 2003.
Hill, John, and Pamela Church Gibson. *The Oxford Guide to Film
    Studies.* New York: Oxford University Press, 1998.
Kaplan, Mike, ed. *Variety International Showbusiness Reference.*
    New York: Garland, 1981.
Katz, Ephraim. *The Film Encyclopedia.* 4th ed. New York: Harper-
    Collins, 2001.
Konigsberg, Ira. *The Complete Film Dictionary.* 2nd ed. New York:
    Penguin, 1997.
Kozarski, Richard, ed. *Hollywood Directors, 1914–1940.* New York:
    Oxford University Press, 1976.
Kozarski, Richard, ed. *Hollywood Directors, 1941–1976.* New York:
    Oxford University Press, 1977.
Magill's Survey of Cinema. Englewood Cliffs, N.J.: Magill, 1983–.
    Annual.
Maltin, Leonard. *Leonard Maltin's Movie Encyclopedia.* New York:
    Plume Books, 1994.
Maltin, Leonard, ed. *Movie and Video Guide.* New York: Plume/
    Penguin Books, 1969–. Annual.
The International Motion Picture Almanac. New York: Quigley,
    1928–. Annual.
The New York Times Film Reviews, 1913–1970. 7 vols. New York:
    Arno, 1971.
The New York Times Film Reviews, 1975–2001. 13 vols. New York:
    Routledge, 1988–2001.
Nowell-Smith, Geoffrey. *The Oxford History of World Cinema.* New
    York: Oxford University Press, 1996.
Rajadhyaksha, Anish, and Paul Willemen, eds. *Encyclopedia of
    Indian Cinema.* 2nd rev. ed. London: BFI, 1999.
Roud, Richard, ed. *Cinema: A Critical Dictionary.* New York:
    Viking, 1980.
Sadoul, Georges. *Dictionary of Film Makers.* Trans. and ed. Peter
    Morris. Berkeley: University of California Press, 1972.
Sadoul, Georges. *Dictionary of Films.* Trans. and ed. Peter Morris.
    Berkeley: University of California Press, 1972.
Sarris, Andrew. *The American Cinema: Directors and Directions,
    1929–1968.* New York: Dutton, 1968.
Speed, F. Maurice, and James Cameron-Wilson. *Film Review.*
    London: W. H. Allen, 1966–. Annual.

Steinberg, Cobbett. *Reel Facts: The Movie Book of Records.*
Updated. New York: Vintage, 1982.
Taylor, Richard, et al., eds. *The BFI Companion to Eastern
European and Russian Cinema.* London: BFI, 2000.
Thomas, Nicholas, ed. *The International Dictionary of Films and
Filmmakers.* 2nd ed. 5 vols. Chicago: St. James Press, 1990–94.
Thomson, David. *The New Biographical Dictionary of Film:
Expanded and Updated.* New York: Knopf, 2004.
Willis, John, ed. *Screen World Film Annual.* London: Applause, 1949–.

The most important and up-to-date sources for film research, along
with scholarly books, are journals and magazines. A writer gradually
becomes familiar with the differences among them, learning to judge
which ones will be most helpful for which topics. The essays and reviews
found here provide a range of information: interviews with actors, script-
writers, and directors; background facts on the production of a movie; and
investigations of complex critical issues (the politics or the formal features
of the movie, for instance). A first step in researching articles on a specific
movie or topic is to scan a good index, which will list most of the essays
and reviews on your subject and will indicate the periodicals in which they
are found. Keep in mind, however, that the titles or information you seek
may be located under headings such as "Motion Pictures" or "Movies."

Besides more general indexes, such as the *Guide to Periodical
Literature* and the film section of the *MLA International Bibliography*,
the following are a few of the standard indexes for film research:

Aceto, Vincent J., Jane Graves, and Fred Silva. *Film Literature
Index.* Albany, N.Y.: Filmdex, 1973–. Quarterly.
Batty, Linda. *Retrospective Index to Film Periodicals, 1930–1971.*
New York: R. R. Bowker, 1975.
Bowles, Stephen E., ed. *Index to Critical Film Reviews in British
and American Periodicals, 1930–1972.* New York: Burt Franklin,
1973.
Bowles, Stephen E., ed. *Index to Critical Reviews of Books about
Film, 1930–1972.* New York: Burt Franklin, 1975.
Bowles, Stephen E., ed. *The Film Anthologies Index.* Metuchen,
N.J.: Scarecrow Press, 1994.
Bukalski, Peter J. *Film Research: A Critical Bibliography with
Annotation and Essay.* Boston: G. K. Hall, 1972.
The Film Index: A Bibliography. 3 vols. New York: The Museum of
Modern Art Film Library, 1941–85.
Gerlach, John C., and Gerlach, Lana. *The Critical Index: 1948–1973.*
New York: Teacher's College Press, 1974.

International Index to Film Periodicals (FIAF Index). New York:
 R. R. Bowker, 1972–. Annual.
Kowalski, Rosemary Ribich. *Women and Film: A Bibliography.*
 Metuchen, N.J.: Scarecrow Press, 1976.
MacCann, Richard Dyer, and Edward S. Perry. *The New Film
 Index: A Bibliography of Magazine Articles in English,
 1930–1970.* New York: Dutton, 1974.
Media Review Digest. Ann Arbor, Mich.: Pierian Press, 1970–.
 Annual.
Monaco, James, and Susan Schenker, eds. *Books about Film: A
 Bibliographical Checklist.* 3rd ed. New York: Zoetrope, 1976.
Rehrauer, George. *The Macmillan Film Bibliography.* 2 vols.
 London: Macmillan, 1982.
Schuster, Mel. *Motion Picture Directors: A Bibliography of
 Magazine and Periodical Articles, 1900–1972.* Metuchen, N.J.:
 Scarecrow Press, 1973.

When consulting these indexes, it is best to begin with more recent
years and then move back through the years to find relevant essays; the
more current articles often have more up-to-date information. Noting the
entries over a period of several years is usually a good start. A just-released
movie, however, may not even appear in the most current index, and in
this case, you must examine the tables of contents of the most recent journals and the movie reviews in newspapers that have appeared in the past
few months. (Some journals, such as *Cinema Journal* and *Film Quarterly,*
feature regular listings or reviews of very recent articles and books about
film.) *Caution:* Invariably, an index will use extreme abbreviations for the
journals; be certain to check the key to those abbreviations before leaving
the index.

Film journals vary considerably in quality and focus, and the
following list of titles indicates the variety and range of journals that
a film researcher will encounter. Some journals offer difficult theoretical essays, others have mainly interviews and short review articles,
and still others (like *Variety*) are a regular source of trade and industry
information. Although those marked with an asterisk feature articles
particularly useful to college students, you should investigate all that
seem to deal with your topic. By using them, you will become familiar
with their advantages and limitations. In addition to these more specialized periodicals, most magazines and newspapers, such as *Newsweek*
or the *New York Times,* are regular sources for movie reviews and
short, general articles. Journals are also becoming more readily available electronically, either through online subscriptions directly with the

journal publisher or through intermediaries, such as library databases like *Project Muse*. Check with your library for a listing of journals available to students online. In addition, many journals have their own websites that frequently include tables of contents for back issues and even sample articles.

In the following list, journals marked with an asterisk are especially recommended:

°Adaptation (http://www.adaptation.oxfordjournals.org). Theoretical, critical, and review essays concerned with the exchanges between literature and film, as well as other forms of cinematic adaptation [two issues annually].

American Cinematographer (http://www.theasc.com/magazine). Short essays and industry information [monthly].

American Film. Review articles and short essays [1975–92].

Bright Lights Film Journal (http://www.brightlightsfilm.com). Review articles, short essays, and film festival and book reviews [online only].

°Cahiers du Cinéma (http://www.cahiersducinema.com). Theoretical essays, current film reviews, and occasional interviews [monthly, French].

°Camera Obscura (http://cameraobscura.dukejournals.org/). Theoretical and feminist essays on film, television, and popular culture [three issues annually].

°Cineaste (http://www.cineaste.com). Critical essays (usually directed at ideological issues), interviews, and current film reviews [quarterly].

°Cinefex (http://www.cinefex.com/magazine.html). Focuses on special-effects technology in the cinema [quarterly].

°Cinema Journal (http://muse.jhu.edu/journals/cj). Critical essays [quarterly].

°Cinema Scope (http://www.cinema-scope.com). Critical essays on international cinema [five issues annually].

°Film Criticism. Critical essays, reviews, and special issues on topics such as feminist film criticism and filmmakers such as Douglas Sirk [three times annually].

°Film Comment (http://www.filmlinc.com/fcm/fcm.htm). Critical essays and reviews of current films, film festivals, and DVD releases [bimonthly].

° Film Philosophy (http://www.film-philosophy.com/archive). An international journal with a wide range of book reviews, theoretical essays, and sophisticated analyses of individual films.

Film Quarterly (http://www.filmquarterly.org). Critical essays, occasional interviews, and current film reviews [quarterly].

Film Reader. Critical essays [1975–85].

Filmfacts. Short reviews of current films [1958–77].

Films and Filming. Short articles and current film reviews [1954–1990].

Framework (http://www.frameworkonline.com). Theoretical and critical essays [biannual].

Frauen und Film. Theoretical and critical essays, feminist emphasis [quarterly, German].

Images: Journal of film and popular culture (http://www.imagesjournal.com). Review articles, short essays, and interviews [online only].

Iris. Critical and theoretical essays [irregularly, French and English].

Journal of Film and Video (http://www.press.uillinois.edu/journals/jfv. html). Critical essays on film, television, and video [quarterly].

Journal of Popular Film and Television (http://www.heldref.org/jpft.php). Critical essays on film and television from a cultural-studies viewpoint [quarterly].

Jump Cut (http://www.ejumpcut.org). Critical essays often directed to political and ideological issues, current film reviews, some interviews [online only].

Literature/Film Quarterly (http://www.salisbury.edu/lfq). Critical essays on topics related to the intersections of film and literature [quarterly].

Midnight Eye (http://www.midnighteye.com). Essays, film and book reviews, and interviews focusing on contemporary Japanese cinema.

Millennium Film Journal (http://mfj-online.org). Theoretical and critical essays focusing on independent, experimental, and avant-garde film and video [irregularly].

Offscreen (http://www.offscreen.com). An online film journal that covers genres, directors, and individual films, along with reviews of festivals and other journals.

Persistence of Vision. Critical and theoretical essays [1984–97].

Positif. Critical and theoretical essays [monthly, French].

Quarterly Review of Film and Video (http://www.tandf.co.uk/journals/ titles/10509208.asp). Critical essays on film and media [quarterly].

Rouge (http://www.rouge.com.au). An international film journal with film critiques, interviews, and broader topics by a spectrum of film scholars.

° *Scope* (http://www.scope.nottingham.ac.uk/index.php). Journal of the Institute of Film Studies at the University of Nottingham containing critical essays, film reviews, scholarly book reviews, and conference reports [online only].

° *Screen* (http://www.gla.ac.uk/services/screen). Critical and theoretical essays [quarterly].

° *Senses of Cinema* (http://www.sensesofcinema.com). Critical essays, current film reviews, film festival reviews, and interviews [online only].

° *Sight and Sound* (http://www.bfi.org.uk/sightandsound). Critical essays and current film reviews [monthly].

Variety (http://www.variety.com). Short articles with current film-industry and commercial information [online and print].

Vectors: Journal of Culture and Technology in a Dynamic Vernacular (http://www.vectorsjournal.org). A conceptually innovative journal that combines scholarship and analysis with new design and delivery technologies.

° *Velvet Light Trap* (http://www.utexas.edu/utpress/journals/jvlt. html). Critical essays [quarterly].

° *Wide Angle* (http://muse.jhu.edu/journals/wide_angle). Critical and theoretical essays [quarterly].

FILM RESEARCH ON THE INTERNET

The Internet is a growing source of research materials, although the quality of that material varies greatly. For students who use the Internet, the World Wide Web system offers discussion groups, access to various library and media catalogs, and numerous specific sites where one can browse for information, such as the Hong Kong Movie page, the Internet Movie Database page, or the pages of the journal *Film Comment*. Services such as Yahoo! offer live video clips, and numerous sites provide still images from films that may be downloaded and printed. Because the sources and information available on the Internet promise to proliferate rapidly, they will offer unique research possibilities. Already, films are being made exclusively for distribution and viewing on the Internet, and videotapes and DVDs of films, otherwise difficult to find, can be rented through Internet sites, such as Facets Video.

Although Internet research is fast becoming a common way to do research on movies, writers need to be especially cautious about the kind of material found online. The fastest, simplest, and consequently often the preferred route is simply to choose a search engine, such as Google,

Yahoo!, or Excite, and type in the title of the film or the topic you wish to research, such as *"127 Hours* (2010)" or "Turkish cinema." Although this is a quick start, the result of your search can offer many possible sites and sources of vastly different quality. There are basically four kinds of research content available on the Internet:

- Some websites and databases offer fundamental facts about a film and the individuals involved with that film, such as the actors or director.
- Some websites may offer complete reviews or critical essays from refereed or academic journals. This material will have been read and evaluated by experts in the field and judged to make important contributions to our understanding of the subject.
- Many websites, listservs, and discussion groups will have no authority or credentials. Because anyone can potentially create or enter these sites, the information found there could be little more than someone's opinion or personal bias.
- Almost every major film now released has its own website. Likewise, virtually every studio and distributor has a website. The information here can range from production facts to gossip and usually contains links to reviews and interviews.

Most libraries will feature databases that organize film titles and resources and can be accessed through a personal computer. Some of these are open to the public; some are limited to subscribers or students at that institution. In addition, many useful Internet sites have information that ranges from stories about stars and recent movie reviews to bibliographies and theoretical essays. The following are representative of this range (keep in mind that these URL addresses sometimes change, grow obsolete, or need adjusting):

General
All Movie Guide (http://www.allmovie.com). Provides film and video reviews and production credits, cross-referenced by actor, director, and genre

Cinema Sites (http://www.cinema-sites.com). A comprehensive listing of links to hundreds of cinema sites

Internet Movie Database (http://www.imdb.com). Provides detailed information on film industry, movie credits, plot summaries, and movie reviews

Professional and Academic
American Film Institute (http://www.afi.com). Offers recent industry news, film events and festivals, educational seminars, and graduate degrees

Berkeley Film Studies Resources (http://www.lib.berkeley.edu/MRC).
A collection of online bibliographies and sources for film and
media studies

Early Cinema.com (http://www.earlycinema.com). An introduction
to the filmmakers, technologies, and social environments for
early cinema, including suggestions for further research

Film Literature Index (http://webapp1.dlib.indiana.edu/fli/index.
jsp). A standard index of the publications in 150 film and media
journals with more than 2,000 subject heads

The Internet Archive (http://www.archive.org). An online digital
library of Internet sites and other digital practices in digital
form for researchers, historians, scholars, and the general public

New York State Archives Motion Picture Scripts Collection (http://
www.archives.nysed.gov/a/research/res_topics_film.shtml).
Provides a fully searchable collection of film scripts that are
available free of charge for academic use

Oxford Bibliographies Online (http://www.oxfordbibliographiesonline.
com). Offers annotated and regularly updated bibliographies on a
wide variety of key topics in film and media studies

ScreenSite (http://www.screensite.org). Provides data on films,
film conferences, archives, and useful links to other academic
cinema sites

Society for Cinema and Media Studies (http://www.cmstudies.org).
Academic society dedicated to the scholarly study of film, television,
and new media

Yale University Library Research Guide in Film Studies (http://
http://guides.library.yale.edu/film). An introductory guide to
conducting library and Internet research in film studies

When using the Internet for research, students need to distinguish
substantial and useful material from chat and frivolous commentary. Especially
with Internet sources, there are important rules of thumb to follow:

- Explore your own library's databases to see what is available there.
This is a quick way to scan titles of film books that bear on your
topic. Remember, however, that these databases may contain
titles that appeared only after a certain date, and they should be
supplemented with a search of the library catalog.
- Determine the quality of the Internet source in providing reliable
information or carefully evaluated argument and research. Is it from
a refereed publication or a reputable institution? Is its information
supported by references to other research? What are the credentials
of the author?

- Define your search as precisely as possible. Beyond just the title of a film, focus your search on, for example, "lighting in Julie Taymor's *The Tempest* (2010)" or "politics, new Iranian cinema, and Bahman Ghobadi's *Turtles Can Fly* (2004)." Pursue your topic through an "advanced search."
- Explore links to other sites. Does your investigation of a specific film link you to sites that discuss other films by that director or related issues (for instance, about the film genre or about the country in which the film was made)?
- Bookmark the site and make a copy of the material that you intend to use, dating when you accessed that material and any other important information.

TAKING NOTES ON SECONDARY SOURCES

Taking notes on secondary sources requires judgment. If you have an idea or a topic firmly in mind as you begin to read, you will need to decide what supports, challenges, or complicates that idea. If you are still trying to clarify your own argument, you will need to read with an open but discriminating mind that allows you to be guided by other opinions while being critical of opinions with which you do not agree. Often, reading a good essay on a film provides the one sentence or paragraph that crystallizes your own idea about the movie and points you down your own path. Be open to suggestions and be willing to follow leads, whether they are ideas or other sources.

When possible, quickly skim or read the essay or chapter first to get a general idea. Then, if it seems noteworthy, read it again. Especially with complex essays (or even books), try to focus and summarize your reading by doing the following:

- Identifying succinctly the main point or points
- Isolating what you consider the one or two most important passages or sentences
- Formulating one or more questions you have about the essay (about, for instance, what you did not understand or what you may disagree with)

Begin, then, to take exact notes on the reading (even in the age of computers, many writers still use four-by-six-inch cards and write on only one side of the card). In taking notes, it may help to identify and organize material that relates to a specific topic or idea (for instance, by creating separate files on your computer or by placing a subject heading at the top of each card to help you sort the cards according to the logic of your paper). Once you have a sense of an article or a chapter, use some of these guidelines in transferring the material to your note cards or files:

1. Summarize ideas from a section of your source, or quote exactly the sentences or passages that may prove useful. If you use an exact quotation, place it in quotation marks. Whether you summarize or quote, be certain to indicate all the necessary information about the source, including the page numbers.

2. When quoting sentences or passages directly, be discriminating. Do not simply copy long paragraphs that seem important but that you have not entirely digested or understood. If you consider carefully the passages that may be helpful to your argument later, the research will help refine your argument at an early stage. No one incorporates every note or summary gathered from secondary sources into the final draft. If you use judgment and reflect on the material you are choosing, however, you will not be faced with a massive pile of notes that have scattered rather than clarified your ideas.

3. Never change occasional words from a quoted passage and copy it as if it were a summary. If that passage appears in your essay, it will look very much like plagiarism.

4. Sometimes, it is advantageous to omit words or phrases from a quotation because they are not relevant to your point. When you do this, indicate the omission with ellipses (three spaced periods).

5. Whether you are summarizing or quoting directly, you may wish to jot down your response to the material, such as, "Galperin is the only critic to recognize how literary this movie is." Be sure to mark off these reflections clearly from the quoted or summarized passage with either brackets or double parentheses.

WRITING THE PAPER

Once you have done your preliminary research, you will move toward a polished essay by integrating that research into a finished draft of your argument. Normally, research papers are anywhere from two thousand to six thousand words (eight to twenty-four double-spaced, typed pages), and the writer should always make the amount and kind of research fit the length of the essay. Here are some guidelines:

1. Begin by rereading the notes you have taken and sorting them into categories, such as "historical background material" or "themes." Not all the information you have gathered will necessarily be useful as you begin to focus your topic. A good writer learns to differentiate between what is truly useful and what is not. Overloading your essay with an enormous number of quotations will not improve it; needless information will only bury your argument. If you have already sketched an outline, now is the time to rework it in light of your research. This reworking of the outline may involve only fine tuning, such as adding some transition sections or expanding a section. Or you may have to rethink your most important premise, shifting and restructuring it to account for some of your recent findings. If your original approach was based on auteurist presumptions that are out of line with the limited control the director had over the particular film, the facts require you to reformulate your argument. As you develop your ideas for this first draft, you should be able to state a fairly clear and precise thesis for the paper.

2. Write, type, or print out your quotations exactly as they will appear in your final draft. Put short quotations (four lines or less) between quotation marks and run them into your text. Longer quotations are not enclosed within quotation marks; instead, they are indented and separated from your prose by a triple space. *Be certain that you have copied the quotations accurately.*

3. Add to your quotations all relevant bibliographical information. This material will appear later in your list of works cited, but it is advantageous to have it before you so that you can easily identify the source when you do your final draft.

4. Get all titles, dates, and technical information right at this point. Include the date the film was released in parentheses next to the title. If you intend to use both the foreign-language title and the English title, be sure to double-check both. When using an author's name in your text, give the full name as it appears in the article, book, or review. In subsequent references to this author, use just the last name (it is unnecessary in most cases to use a title like *Professor* or *Ms*).

5. This early draft may also be the best place to write out concrete descriptions of the shots or sequences to which you refer. When your points require the use of other films as examples, consider and insert those titles.

6. When you revise this draft, introduce your research and quotations with a lead-in so that you get the most from them. Cramming all your research into one section or introducing each quotation with "A says" or "B says" (or, worse yet, no introductory phrase at all) suggests that you have not considered carefully how best to use your research. A good rhetorical strategy is to let the reader know *why* you are using the material by remarking, "In this perceptive review of the film..." or "A typical but superficial response to the movie is summed up in this comment..." Sometimes short remarks or phrases can be integrated directly into your prose and simply annotated:

> The closing is, as one writer put it, "a confusing assault on the viewer" (King 121).

If you are contrasting interpretations, make that clear in the way you use and introduce the quotations or paraphrases. You might lead into the quotations thus: "Consider two opposing views of Woo's use of flashbacks here." In the end, your readers should feel not only that they have read a specific and well-formulated argument, but also that it is based on sound judgments about the film, the facts surrounding the film, and the perceptions of other knowledgeable viewers.

7. If your last draft is easy to read, it will be much easier to revise on the computer screen.

8. After you have printed out a final draft of the essay, check the titles, dates, and page numbers of all your bibliographical information. Be sure you have included all the works used in the works-cited section (pp. 165–168) and, if you choose to, all the works you consulted (but, perhaps, did not use) in a works-consulted section (p. 165).

9. Be certain to save and back up your work on your computer and make an extra copy of it before submitting the paper in case the original is lost or misplaced by you or your instructor.

SAMPLE ESSAYS

The following are two versions of the same essay: One relies on an intelligent writer's careful reflection on the movie; the other develops that knowledge through a moderate amount of research. Both versions are competent, but the second carries a rhetorical force and authority that distinguish it from the first. Notice also how research does more than just support the original ideas; it helps the writer to develop those ideas further and even to change their direction.

Images of Violence in Penn's *Bonnie and Clyde*

Arthur Penn's *Bonnie and Clyde* (1967) is basically a gangster movie which glorifies the lives of Bonnie Parker and Clyde Barrow, two young criminals on the run in the thirties. Thematically, one of the most striking features of the film is how these small-time hoodlums become larger-than-life heroes in a society that seems to be crumbling in every way. Stylistically, the film is also remarkable. Through a number of stunning shots, which culminate in the grotesque killing of the pair at the conclusion of the film, the movie seems constantly to call attention to itself as a movie about image making. Integrating these themes and style in a gripping and suspenseful story, *Bonnie and Clyde* is an unusual and perplexing movie about the bizarre relationship between two people's desperate need to escape the daily miseries of their society and the violence that is necessary for that escape.

One of the unusual variations in this gangster film is that the heroes (or antiheroes) are also victims, clownish drifters who become involved in a life of crime mainly because they need an identity of one sort or another (Figure 6.02). These public enemies never seem to demonstrate any of the real malice or the professional confidence that is associated with a gangster of the James Cagney variety. Through the work of carefully framed and emptied shots, the land they live in seems a wasteland, the people they encounter mostly sad and poor. Bonnie joins Clyde in her first robbery attempt because she is bored, lonely, and looking for some excitement, and in a later scene, Clyde seems shocked and confused that one of his victims should actually defend himself by trying to kill Clyde.

Handwritten margin notes:

gives some background about story and introduces argument in thesis

Thesis

Bonnie & Clyde aren't the typical gangsters

(6.)

Figure 6.02 The desperadoes of *Bonnie and Clyde* (1967): gangsters, or politicians?

More important, as the film progresses, these two gangsters seem motivated more by the wish to see their names and pictures in the paper than by a wish to accumulate large amounts of money (which is rarely discussed by the gang). When Clyde's brother, Buck, comes to visit, Bonnie and Clyde have their pictures taken in the theatrical pose of gangsters, and for them, this kind of exaggerated image of themselves—mostly in the paper and the public's imagination—is what allows them to have a real identity in their depression-ravaged society. Summing up their true reason for their violent life of crime, Clyde convinces Bonnie to join him by exclaiming, "Everybody'd know about us!"

In this sense, these two criminals are not just victims of their society (an old cliché) but victims of the sensationalism which they need and which the press panders to. (This seems more true today than it possibly could have in the thirties.) In a way, their need for those glossy images of themselves is what seals their fate, since it is their humiliation of the Texas Ranger with a newspaper photo that motivates him to hunt them down. Ultimately, to put this succinctly, they are trapped in the logic of their desire for glorious self-images, just as toward the end of the film, Clyde is—tragically and comically—unable to envision a different kind of life, but only different tactics for robbing banks.

by getting their names in the paper they sealed their fate to be caught

The sensational climax and conclusion of the movie are consequently entirely appropriate. That the death of the two "heroes" follows a scene in which they read Bonnie's poetic description of their adventures and then make love for the first time is a summary statement of the movie's logic. When Clyde reads the ballad, he says, "You've told our story.... You've made us somebody." They have found, in short, the identities and public images they have been searching for, and they are now able to consummate their love. The slow-motion, multiangled death that follows can be seen, moreover, as an extension of their newfound identities. Trapped in the logic of sensationalism and public images, they, in the end, find themselves only in the sensational movie images in which they die.

She concludes that their silly obsession of being famous has only gotten them the silly movie where they die.

Katherine Smith

Images of Violence in Penn's *Bonnie and Clyde*

Although *Bonnie and Clyde* (1967) still retains much of its original power, it may be difficult for contemporary audiences to appreciate fully the impact of this extremely successful movie. In his *History of Narrative Film,* David Cook summarizes the tumultuous reception of this tumultuous movie:

Takes a different argument

A new American cinema and a new American film audience announced themselves emphatically with the release in 1967 of Arthur Penn's *Bonnie and Clyde*. This film, which was universally attacked by the critics when it opened in August, had by November become the most popular film of the year. It would subsequently receive ten Academy Awards nominations and win two…, win the New York Film Critics' Award for Best Script…and be named the Best Film of 1967 by many of the critics who had originally panned it. Most triumphant of all, perhaps, Bonnie and Clyde is the only film ever to have forced the public retraction of a critical opinion by Time magazine….Indeed, the phenomenal success of Bonnie and Clyde caused many retractions on the part of veteran film critics who, on first viewing, had mistaken it for a conventional bloody, gangster film. (626)

There is, of course, no denying that the movie is basically a bloody descendant of the 1930s when, according to a 1934 FBI report, Bonnie and Clyde instigated "one of the most colorful and spectacular manhunts the Nation had seen up to that time" (1). Through its documentary style and the old photos used during the credit sequence, Penn's film seems to present itself as a portrait of the thirties. But the confused initial response to the movie indicates, I believe, that there is something more going on: that Penn, through the self-conscious style he supposedly learned from the French New Wave,[1] is offering a complicated commentary on modern images of violence in America and a disturbing critique of how Americans have escaped into those images, especially during the sixties.

[1]The influence of directors like Godard, Truffaut, and Chabrol on Penn and other American directors is often remarked in film histories. In general, these new, confrontational styles began to make their appearance in the United States in the mid-1960s.

There are several signs that this is more than a gangster film and about more than the 1930s. Most notably, in this gangster film, the heroes (or antiheroes) also seem to be victims, clownish drifters who become involved in a life of crime mainly because they need an identity of one sort or another. These public enemies never seem to demonstrate any of the real malice or the professional confidence associated with the James Cagney variety of gangster; likewise, the world they live in lacks all the glamour of a gangster's world. Through the work of carefully framed and emptied shots, the land they drive through seems a wasteland, the people they encounter mostly sad and poor. Bonnie joins Clyde in her first robbery attempt because she is bored, lonely, and looking for some excitement, and in a later scene, Clyde seems shocked and confused that one of his victims should actually defend himself by trying to kill Clyde.

T.S.

uses same ￠ as first essay to say gangsters are victims

More important, as the film progresses, these two gangsters seem motivated more by the wish to see their names and pictures in the paper than by a wish to accumulate large amounts of money (which is rarely discussed by the gang). When Clyde's brother, Buck, comes to visit, Bonnie and Clyde have their pictures taken in the theatrical poses of gangsters, and for them, these kinds of exaggerated images of themselves—mostly found in the papers and the public's imagination—are what allows them to have a real identity apart from their depression-ravaged society. Summing up their true reason for their violent life of crime, Clyde convinces Bonnie to join him by exclaiming, "Everybody'd know about us!" These two criminals are not just victims of their society (an old cliché) but victims of the sensationalism which they need and which the press panders to.

T.S.

Same ￠ to say that they wanted to be famous

This connection between violence and publicity seems to me to make *Bonnie and Clyde* as much about the late sixties as about the thirties. In the late sixties, when the violence of Vietnam was on everyone's television screen, the media were pandering to and

new ￠ to say the film isn't just about '30s but also '60s *T.S.*

creating sensational violence as never before.[2] As Pauline Kael has perceptively observed, although the "Vietnam war has barely been mentioned on the screen,…you can feel it in *Bonnie and Clyde*" (225). Where an audience can most specifically see and feel that war is, I believe, not only in the large amounts of graphic violence in the film but, more significantly, in the way the movie logically links its violence to the sensationalism of the media coverage. In a way, Bonnie and Clyde's need for glossy images of themselves is what motivates them and what seals their fate, since it is their humiliation of the Texas Ranger with a newspaper photo that results in his relentlessly hunting them down. They are trapped in the violent logic of their desire for glorious self-images—just as toward the end of the movie, Clyde is (tragically and comically) unable to envision a different kind of life but only different tactics for robbing banks.

[handwritten margin note: violence is connected and so is media coverage to the audiences lives]

Bonnie and Clyde, in short, are neither simply thirties gangsters surviving through crime nor sixties rebels searching for identities. They are mindless participants in a glorious and violent sensationalism, the same sensationalism with which the public media created a confused national identity during the war-torn sixties.

[handwritten margin note: Its new ¶ B & C are used]

The sensational climax and conclusion are consequently entirely appropriate in a film about the search for identity in a violent society. That the death of the two "heroes" follows scenes in which they read Bonnie's poetic description of their adventure in the newspaper and then make love for the first time is a summary statement of the film's logic. When Clyde reads the ballad, he says, "You've told our story.…You've made us somebody." They have found, in short, the identities and public images they have been searching for, and they are now able to consummate their love. The slow-motion, multiangled death that follows can be seen,

[handwritten margin note: ¶S]
[handwritten margin note: Same ¶ to say their logic was silly]

---

[2]The ambiguous but unprecedented role of the public media in the Vietnam War is probably best summed up by the common observation that it was "the first war fought on television."

moreover, as an extension of that newfound identity. Trapped in the logic of violent sensationalism and public images, they aptly find themselves only in the violent and sensational movie images in which they die.

As an indirect image of the sixties, *Bonnie and Clyde* may not be, however, as much a statement of despair as it seems. If Bonnie and Clyde are trapped, Penn's movie may have worked to untrap its 1967 audience through its self-conscious and graphic assault on them. Like the French New Wave directors, Penn may have been attempting to make his audience consider more actively the violent images through which they lived. In that sense, the confused and contradictory response to *Bonnie and Clyde* may be an indication that it achieved its aim.

The thesis is answered and more questions are raised

Works Cited

Cook, David. *A History of Narrative Film.* New York: Norton, 1981.

Federal Bureau of Investigation Freedom of Information Act Electronic Reading Room. 3 March 2000 http://foia.fbi.gov/bonclyd.html.

Kael, Pauline. *Reeling.* New York: Warner Books, 1972.

Exercises

1. Locate three different kinds of research sources for a specific film topic: one from a scholarly journal, one from a book, and one from the Internet. Write a paragraph on each, evaluating their individual strengths and weaknesses.

2. Select two passages from two different research sources dealing with a specific film. Write a paragraph on each passage succinctly summarizing the point of the passage and detailing why you agree or disagree with the position of that passage.

7

MANUSCRIPT FORM

MANUSCRIPT COPY

Although every instructor has individual expectations and requirements about the final form in which an essay should be submitted, all writers follow general guidelines when putting an essay into its final form:

1. Print out a clean copy of your paper. A cleanly printed manuscript simply looks more professional and is usually easier to read. A professional appearance gives you an edge with your reader, who will see your work from the beginning as something you took seriously. Some writers find that a hard copy of the paper allows them to read and revise their work from a new perspective. When you have the time and the word-processing skills, it is a real advantage to revise a printed draft before making your final revisions.

2. Use clean 8.5-by-11-inch paper, printed on one side, with sharp, easily readable print.

3. Most instructors prefer that you put your name, date, and perhaps the course number on three lines in the right-hand corner of the first page. Separate title pages are normally unnecessary.

4. It is not necessary to number the first page, but be certain to number all the following pages. Usually, page numbers appear at the top of each page in the middle or the right-hand corner. Numbers centered at the bottom of the page are also acceptable.

5. Leave uniform and adequate margins on each page: an inch or an inch and a half on both sides and at the top and the bottom of the page. It is silly to think that larger margins will somehow disguise a short paper.

6. Double-space all the copy, except for long quotes, which are indented and single-spaced. (The Modern Language Association [MLA] guide says to double-space even the long, indented passages, but this practice is used mainly for professional essays being submitted to journals.)

7. Center your title two inches (twelve lines) from the top of the first page. Begin your essay one inch below the title. Capitalize the first letter of each word in your title, except prepositions, articles, and conjunctions.

Underline or italicize only the titles of films that appear in your title. Do not underline or use quotation marks around any other part of your title, unless that part comes from another source and requires these punctuation marks. Thus a standard title would appear like this:

Conrad, Coppola, and *Apocalypse Now*

When you use a quotation from another source within your title, the quoted material appears in quotation marks:

Versions of a *Heart of Darkness:*

"The Horror, the Horror" of *Apocalypse Now*

When a title does not fit easily on one line, a second line is preferable to crowding a title within the width of a page. The second line should also be centered.

8. Indent each new paragraph five spaces from the left margin.

9. Most instructors do not expect stills to accompany your essay, nor is it an especially good idea to include a showy still that serves no greater purpose than to dress up your paper. When an essay is focused on a single shot or a series of shots, however, it may be helpful to reproduce a still or a series of stills in an appendix at the end of your paper. If you can obtain a pertinent still (or stills), be sure that it is reproduced and labeled clearly, that you identify its place in the film when you discuss it in your text, and that you refer explicitly to the reproduction at that point:

In *Apocalypse Now,* the insane theatrics of politics crystallize in the Playboy Bunny Show deep in the jungle (see Appendix 1).

10. Always back up a copy of your final draft or make a copy of your essay to keep in case your original is lost or misplaced.

11. Staple your paper in the upper-left-hand corner.

LAST-MINUTE CORRECTIONS

Writers are prone to making last-minute revisions or corrections. After your paper is in its final printed form, corrections should be kept to a minimum, because too many penciled-in changes will destroy the desired effect of a cleanly typed manuscript. As you proofread your final copy, however, you might discover small errors, misspellings, and typographical mistakes, and you can correct these neatly by using proofreading symbols and markings. Better yet: print out a newly corrected copy.

To add a word or a phrase, use a caret in the appropriate space:

```
                              film
    Before 1917, Russian∧culture was mainly
    European.
```

Transpositions of letters or words are done in this way:

```
    Before 1917, Russian fl⁀im culture mainly⁀was
    European.
```

To separate words that are mistakenly run together, insert a vertical line; close unnecessary gaps with a curved line connecting the letters that need to be joined:

```
    Before 1917, Russian fil‿m culture was⁄mainly
    European.
```

A final proofreading may reveal a paragraph that should be broken into two paragraphs. Use the paragraph symbol to indicate where a new paragraph should start:

```
    Many do not even consider Russian movies before
    ¶revolutionary figures like Vertov and Eisenstein.
     Before 1917 Russian Film culture was mainly
    European.
```

When one or two words are incorrect, you can easily change them by simply crossing out the wrong words or letters and printing the necessary corrections above them:

```
                                 was
    Before 1917, Russian film culture w̶e̶r̶e̶ mainly
    European.
```

QUOTATIONS

In writing about film, you will have to deal with two kinds of quotations:

1. In quoting dialogue or commentary from the film itself, normally no footnotes are necessary, and the words quoted can be integrated directly into your text.

2. In quoting from essays, books, or interviews with individuals involved in the production, you need some kind of footnote and documentation. If these quotations are short passages, they, too, can be inserted directly into your prose:

> One prominent critic has described this film as "a study in postmodern emptiness."

Whether the paper is short or long has little to do with the use of quotations, but when quotations are used, they should be punctuated properly and spread judiciously throughout the essay (never make your essay a string of quotations). The following are some general guidelines:

1. Whatever you are quoting, be accurate and check the quoted passages when you proofread. In most cases, quotations should correspond exactly to the original in spelling, capitalization, and punctuation. When you add material within the quotation, put those words in brackets. When you underline a word or phrase to emphasize it, note that it is your emphasis in parentheses after the quotation:

> Many factors distinguished the American studios of the thirties, but, in the words of one historian, "The hierarchy of American studios [in the thirties] was in some crucial ways determined by the *class* of audience they targeted" (Venuti 122, my emphasis).

If you need or wish to omit unnecessary words within a quoted passage, signal the omission with three spaced periods, called *ellipsis points:*

> In the words of one historian, "The hierarchy of American studios was... determined by the class of audience they targeted" (Venuti 122).

Ellipsis points are not needed at the very beginning or end of a sentence. If the ellipsis ends a sentence in the middle of a quoted passage, include a period at the end of that sentence, then three periods for the ellipsis.

2. Do not use quoted passages to make your points for you or to take up large blocks of space. Use them to support your points.

3. If you are quoting a long piece of dialogue from a movie or an exchange between two characters, this quotation is usually single-spaced and indented rather than put in quotation marks in your text:

BERNARD: First of all, not all women. And secondly you frighten me. Sometimes you looked at me severely, and even with a certain hostility.

MARION: With a certain hostility? Really?

Passages longer than four lines of typescript or print should also be indented without quotation marks. When you indent to quote dialogue or long passages, triple-space before and after the quote, and either single-space or double-space the passage, depending on the preference of your instructor. Most professional publications ask that these passages be double-spaced like the rest of the manuscript, but for most student research papers, a single-spaced passage looks better.

4. Introduce your quotations; never end one sentence and begin the next sentence with an unannounced quotation. Most commonly, this means acknowledging the speaker or source of the passage with a phrase such as

André Bazin comments:...

or

As Kracauer has argued in *Theory of Film*,...

For quotations that are especially important to your argument or that may be a bit difficult to relate to your point, a nearby phrase or sentence can rephrase the central point so that it is not missed:

The debate about the relation of the film image and physical reality becomes an explicitly social and metaphysical issue in the work of André Bazin. As he says,...

5. When integrating quotations into your own sentences, make them as succinct as possible and adjust them to fit the grammar and syntax of your prose. At times, you may wish to use brackets to insert your own language into the middle of a quotation (as in item 1 in the list on pp. 158).

6. In American usage, periods and commas are placed inside the quotation marks; colons and semicolons are placed outside. Exclamation points, question marks, and dashes are placed inside the quotation marks when they appear as part of the original passage and outside when they are part of your sentence.

7. When there is a quotation within the quote you are using, use single quotation marks for the inner quotation:

> "The most provocative and problematic statement in Kracauer's work is 'the redemption of physical reality.'"

If this embedded quotation were part of an indented passage, it would appear with double quotation marks because the block of indented sentences is not enclosed within quotation marks.

8. Double quotation marks are used to set off the titles of shorter works, such as essays, articles, short poems, and songs. Underline or italicize titles of movies, books, long poems, albums, plays, and paintings. Whether a movie is short or long, its title is italicized. The title of a screenplay is italicized. The titles of television series are italicized; episodes of those series are in quotation marks.

ACKNOWLEDGING SOURCES

When writing an essay, you must maintain a clear sense of what is your own thinking and what is borrowed from others. Acknowledging and noting other perceptions and comments never diminishes the quality or strength of your paper; on the contrary, those acknowledgments strengthen and legitimize your ideas by placing them in the context of other work. Problems arise when, for one reason or another, a reader believes you are not making a clear distinction between your own perceptions and ideas and someone else's. In those instances, the trust between a reader and a writer is broken, and, at the very least, a reader will begin to doubt that the writer truly understands what he or she is saying. A suspicion of plagiarism will undermine all the hard work that has gone into a paper. Consequently, when researching and writing, you must maintain a sure distinction between sentences and words taken directly from another source, paraphrases or summaries of someone else's words, and general ideas appropriated from another source.

Taking the following passage as source material, let us consider the requirements and strategies for using and acknowledging secondary sources:

> The Neorealists were working for a cinema intimately connected with the experience of living: nonprofessional actors, rough technique, political point, ideas rather than entertainment—all these elements went directly counter to the Hollywood esthetic of smooth, seamless professionalism. While Neorealism as a movement lasted only until

the early fifties, the effects of its esthetics are still being felt. In fact, Zavattini, Rossellini, De Sica, and Visconti defined the ground rules that would operate for the next thirty years. Esthetically, Hollywood never quite recovered. (Monaco 253)

1. *Direct quotation.* Phrases from this passage or the entire passage may be taken as needed to make your point. You will introduce the phrases or sentences, place the precise wording within quotation marks, and add the proper references to the work (usually author's name and page number) in parentheses:

> Neorealism was not simply a localized and short-lived phenomenon. As James Monaco puts it, "While Neorealism as a movement lasted only until the early fifties, the effects of its esthetics are still being felt. In fact, Zavattini, Rossellini, De Sica, and Visconti defined the ground rules that would operate for the next thirty years. Esthetically, Hollywood never quite recovered" (253).

The exact form you use when citing the source for a quotation can differ (see pp. 163–165), but some acknowledgment should be made following a direct quotation.

2. *Paraphrasing or summarizing information.* The specific wording of a passage may be less important than the central concept, which a writer might then wish to paraphrase or summarize. To paraphrase from another writer's work means to rephrase sentences so that they fit your prose better; to summarize usually suggests a reduction of the original passage, which nonetheless retains the core of the meaning in the new words. Unless the author writes badly, it is usually better to summarize than to paraphrase. In either case, proper credit must be given to the original source:

> In *How to Read a Film,* James Monaco points out that Italian Neorealists were concerned with living experience and shared basic tenets about filmmaking: nonprofessional actors, an emphasis on ideas and politics, and an unglossy look quite unlike Hollywood's. Especially through the work of individuals like Zavattini, Rossellini, De Sica, and Visconti, the effects of Neorealism were felt for three decades after its first appearance in the late forties, and to some extent Hollywood has never totally recovered from its aesthetic impact (253).

3. *Acknowledging an idea.* Sometimes a writer borrows an idea to use so generally or briefly that it is unnecessary to quote the original or even to paraphrase or summarize it. If you determine that the idea is

original enough that the source deserves mention, be certain to mention it. If you are in doubt, it is better to acknowledge a source than to risk the charge of plagiarism. In an essay on the Hollywood realism of the 1960s, for instance, a writer might note the following in passing:

> Although many consider Hollywood a fairly enclosed world, Neorealism had, as James Monaco has suggested, a definite effect on the Hollywood productions that followed it.

No more formal citation is necessary, except for the listing of Monaco's book in the works-cited section of your paper, yet general acknowledgments such as these prevent any confusion on the part of your reader and often lend authority to your own argument.

NOTE: The information or dialogue you take from a film usually does not need formal acknowledgment as long as you clearly refer to the title of the film that the information comes from. When you are using a script, however, you should acknowledge and document that source. Finally, if you know that there is more than one version of a film circulating—as with *The Man Who Fell to Earth* (1976, 1987) or *M* (1931, 1951)—it is a good idea to specify which version you are using.

Common Knowledge

As you continue to read about, discuss, and write about the movies, you will realize that what you once took for an original idea or insight seems more like common knowledge. This realization is a consequence of your growing understanding of the field. Thus at first you might be inclined to quote or cite an article that remarks that "Italian Neorealism, for all practical purposes, began in 1945 with Rossellini's *Open City*." As you grow more familiar with film and film literature, however, you will realize that this information is standard, can be found in many sources, and does not require attribution. Using it in a later paper, you might decide that there is no need for a formal acknowledgment.

The status of information does change. When a statement first appears, it may be an original proposition; as it becomes assimilated into the critical literature, it gradually becomes common knowledge. There will be judgment calls, when you have to decide whether the information is or is not common knowledge. In the previous passage by James Monaco, a well-read writer would no doubt find it unnecessary to quote or refer to Monaco if he or she noted that Neorealism used unprofessional actors, had an unpolished look, or was based on political commitment. A less well-read writer may feel insecure without making some mention of the source where the statement was first discovered. Again, follow a simple guideline: When in doubt about whether to cite and document a source, do it.

DOCUMENTING SOURCES

Documenting your sources can be a confusing business because there are so many different formats for that documentation. The British, for instance, have traditionally used a slightly different system of punctuation and documentation, and in the United States we have always had a variety of styles and formats to choose from when doing notes. In any given collection of essays or books, one could find an MLA style or a Chicago style of footnotes or endnotes. Although you should ask your instructor whether she or he prefers a particular style, the following is based on the MLA system of documentation and is acceptable in almost all situations.

Two kinds of notes can figure in an essay or a book:

1. Notes that document the source from which a quoted phrase or an idea comes
2. Notes that provide a commentary on some portion of your text or on a quotation you use

Notes for Documentation

In some formats, the writer can document with either footnotes or endnotes, but in the MLA format, only with commentary notes does the writer have that option. Notes used to document a source, in the MLA format, always have a two-part structure: a reference within your text and a list of works cited that completes the documentation at the end of your essay. With notes of this kind, there is no longer a need to number your references. Instead, whenever there is explicit or implicit use of a source, use one of the following methods to acknowledge the source:

1. Cite the author's last name and the page numbers in parentheses at the end of your sentence:

   A recent study has described these stunning images in Ozu's films as "pillow shots" (Burch 160–61).

2. When you use the author's last name in your sentence, use only the page number or numbers of the source in your parentheses:

> Noël Burch has described these stunning images in Ozu's films as
> "pillow shots" (160–61).

3. When you are making a general reference to the work of an author whose name is mentioned in your sentence—rather than a specific reference—omit any parenthetical reference and document the source only in the list of works cited:

> In a study of Japanese cinema for the period 1896–1933, Noël Burch examines the specific discourses of the films and argues convincingly for the distinctive excellence of the early films of Ozu, Mizoguchi, and less well-known masters.

Although this reference is brief and general, it is not complete unless the entire reference to Burch's book is given in the works-cited list.

Note that when the author's name and the page number are included, no punctuation is necessary between the two. Normally, the parentheses come at the end of the sentence and are followed by a period. Only occasionally will you wish to insert the reference at the end of a clause, where it usually would be followed by a comma:

> Although one commentator has argued convincingly for a kind of "pillow shot" in Ozu's films (Burch 160–61), others have debated this designation.

When the reference is a long, indented passage, the parenthetical reference comes after the period at the end of the passage:

> Less concerned with formal innovations, two other critics have praised the later Ozu films and locate their power in their various perspectives on the family structure:

> In every Ozu film the whole world exists in one family. The ends of the earth are no more distant than outside the house. The people are members of a family rather than members of a society, though the family may be in disruption, as in *Tokyo Story,* may be nearly extinct, as in *Late Spring* or *Tokyo Twilight,* or may be a kind of family substitute, the small group in a large company, as in *Early Spring.* (Anderson and Richie 359)

There will be variations on these formulas. If your essay includes references to more than one work by the same author, you must be sure to indicate the title of the appropriate work in your text:

> (Burch, *Theory of Film Practice* 76).

Likewise, if you use authors with the same last name, be certain to give first names or initials in any reference to them. When citing a work written by more than one author, include each name; if there are more than three authors, use the first name followed by *et al.* For books with more than one volume, place the volume number and a colon after the author's name in the parentheses:

(Roud 2: 991)

Works Cited

The list of works cited that appears at the end of your essay gives complete documentation of the works you refer to in any way. Unless your instructor requests it, do not include books or articles that you consulted but did not use. If necessary, you can always follow "Works Cited" with "Works Consulted." Each of these lists should each begin on a new page following your text or endnotes, and the pagination should continue in the same order.

The recently published third edition of the *MLA Style Manual and Guide to Scholarly Publishing*, (2008) suggests several significant changes to documentation and formatting guidelines. These include italicizing, rather than underlining, all titles; adding both issue and volume numbers to all journal entries; and adding the medium of publication (print, web, audio, CD, film, etc.) to every works-cited entry. These guidelines also propose a simplified style for all online citations, without URLs. The model below reflect this revised MLA style.

The title "Works Cited" should be centered at the top of the page (without quotation marks and not underlined). The composition of this list is much like that of a traditional bibliography: last names first, alphabetical order, first line flush with the margin and turnover lines indented five spaces, double-space between entries, and so on. Here, however, are a few other guidelines for the MLA format:

- When you are listing more than one work by the same author, alphabetize the works by title (ignoring initial articles such as *The*). Rather than repeat the author's name after the first entry, use three hyphens where the name would appear.
- Use shortened or abbreviated forms whenever possible: *PA* instead of *Pennsylvania; Little, Brown* instead of *Little, Brown and Company.*
- Do not use a comma between a journal title and a volume number: In this example, 31 represents the volume number, which is separated by a period from the issue number, 2:

Film Quarterly 31.2

- Do not use *p.* or *pp.* to indicate page numbers.
- For periodical articles, use a colon to separate the volume and the year of publication from the specific page numbers:

  Film Quarterly 37.4 (1984): 6–18.

- Use lowercase abbreviations to identify the roles of named writers (such as *ed.* for "editor" or *trans.* for "translator"). When these designations follow a period, capitalize the first letter of the abbreviation.

The following are some examples of typical "Works Cited" entries:

- A book with one author:

  Kozloff, Sarah. *Overhearing Film Dialogue.* Berkeley: U of California P, 2000. Print.

- Two or more books by the same author:

  Andrew, J. Dudley. *Concepts in Film Theory.* New York: Oxford UP, 1984. Print.
  ———. *The Major Film Theories.* New York: Oxford UP, 1976. Print.

- A book by two or more authors:

  Talbot, David, and Barbara Zheutlin. *Creative Differences: Profiles of Hollywood Dissidents.* Boston: South End Press, 1978. Print.

- An edited book:

  James, David, ed. *To Free the Cinema: Jonas Mekas and the New York Underground.* Princeton: Princeton UP, 1992. Print.

- A book with an author and an editor:

  Burch, Noël. *To the Distant Observer: Form and Meaning in the Japanese Cinema.* Ed. Annette Michelson. Berkeley and Los Angeles: U of California P, 1981. Print.

- A work in an anthology:

  Johnston, Claire. "Women's Cinema as Counter-Cinema." *Movies and Methods.* Vol. 1. Ed. Bill Nichols. Berkeley and Los Angeles: U of California P, 1976. 208–17. Print.

- A book that has been translated:

  Burch, Noël. *Theory of Film Practice.* Trans. Helen R. Lane. Princeton, NJ: Princeton UP, 1981. Print.

- A book with more than one volume:

  Agee, James. *Agee on Film.* 2 vols. New York: Grosset and Dunlap, 1958. Print.

- An article in a journal with continuous pagination:

  Brustein, Robert. "Film Chronicles: Reflections on Horror Movies." *Partisan Review* 25.2 (1958): 291. Print.

- An article in a journal that pages each issue separately:

  Petro, Patrice. "Mass Culture and the Feminine: The 'Place' of Television in Film Studies." *Cinema Journal* 25.3 (1986): 5–21. Print.

- Interviews:

  Kurosawa, Akira. Interview. "Making Films for All the People." With Kyoko Hirano. *Cineaste* 14.4 (1986): 23–25. Print.

- Reviews and articles from weekly or daily periodicals or newspapers:

  Sarris, Andrew. "Stranded in Soho's Mean Streets." *The Village Voice* 17 Sept. 1985: 54. Print.

- An article from an online magazine:

  Sragow, Michael. "An Art Wedded to Truth." *Atlantic Monthly.* The Atlantic Monthly, Oct. 1994. Web. 12 Aug. 1997.

- An online professional site:

  American Beauty: The Official Motion Picture Web Site. http://www.americanbeauty-thefilm.com. Web. 5 April 2000.

- An article from an online scholarly journal:

  Thompson, Frank. "Harry Langdon—The Fourth Genius?" *Film Comment* (May/June 1997). Web. 30 March 1999.

When documenting online research, provide as much of the following information as is available: author's name, title of the specific article or text used, title of the publication or site, volume and issue numbers or other identifying numbers, date of publication, page numbers or paragraph numbers, and date of access to the information. Provide URL information only if it is necessary to allow the user to retrieve the content. It is always preferable to print out a copy of the research used.

- Material from a DVD or videotape:

> *Nosferatu.* Dir. F. W. Murnau. Perf. Max Schreck, Alexander Granach, Gustav Von Wangenheim, and Greta Schroeder. 1922. Alpha Video, 2001. DVD.

Always identify whether you are referencing a videocassette or DVD. Include the director, main performers, and original release date of the film, followed by the video/DVD distributor and year.

Notes Supplying Additional Commentary

A writer may wish to insert endnotes or footnotes not to document a passage but to explain or comment on it further. Unless it appears as a footnote at the bottom of the appropriate page, this type of note should appear on a separate page, numbered consecutively and placed between the end of your text and the works-cited page. The heading of the page, centered at the top, should be "Notes" or "Endnotes." The notes should begin five spaces in from the left margin. Numbers corresponding to the numbers in your text should be elevated half a line. When the note runs more than one line, subsequent lines should beg in flush with the margin. Double-space these notes, begin them with a capital letter, and end them with a period.

In general, there are two kinds of endnotes or footnotes: (1) ones that supply additional commentary on a point or remark in your text and (2) ones that refer readers to additional sources:

> Before 1917, Russian film culture was mainly European.[1]

(1)

> [1]Although this statement is accepted by most film historians, recent scholarship suggests that there were other, more indigenous, film cultures beginning to appear in Russia well before 1917.

(2)

> [1]For details and debate about early Russian film culture, see Leyda (3–90) and Taylor (1–20).

Notice that the references and page numbers in the second note are cited in the standard fashion. Those references must then be fully documented in the list of works cited:

Leyda, Jay. *Kino.* 3rd ed. Princeton, NJ: Princeton UP, 1983. Print.

Taylor, Richard. *The Politics of Soviet Cinema, 1917–1929.* New York: Cambridge UP, 1979. Print.

COMMON CONVENTIONS OF USAGE

We are all prone to common errors that may require special attention when we are composing and revising. Some students, for instance, continually confuse *its* and *it's* (the first is a possessive pronoun, like *ours* or *his;* the second is a contraction for *it is*). Others have difficulty with subject–verb agreement and must regularly review and look out for this kind of mistake. Commas, dashes, and hyphens can all become crutches for a writer who is unsure of how they are used to divide or balance sentences and words. These are not trivial concerns in writing, whatever the subject, and every writer must become aware of chronic problems with usage, which can be corrected. The following are a sample of the most typical errors in writing about film.

Names

Always verify the spelling of the names of filmmakers, movie personnel, characters, and actors. Names may have difficult foreign spellings, and care must be taken to get them right. Some names may be accented or hyphenated, and when common usage indicates that initials are used for a first name, such as D. W. Griffith, that usage should be adhered to. In most instances, titles like *Mr., Miss,* or *Ms.* are dropped, and once a full name is introduced in an essay, subsequent references usually use only the last name. Never use simply a first name to feign a casual stance toward a character or actor.

Titles

Full titles of books or films, capitalized and italicized, should be given when they are first referred to, but after that a writer can use a common abbreviation: *The Apprenticeship of Duddy Kravitz* (1974) becomes just *Duddy Kravitz.* It is a good idea to check these titles, because the shortened form frequently becomes the traditional usage (as with Kubrick's *2001*) when the full title offers important information (*2001: A Space Odyssey*).

Whether to use the original foreign-language title or its English translation depends, to some extent, on your instructor. For film courses in foreign-language departments, the original titles will probably be expected; in other courses, the English title will probably suffice. With some titles (such as *Viridiana* [1961] or *Ballet Mécanique* [1924]), the original is used in English also. In some instances, the English title has nothing to do with the original foreign title: Wim Wenders's film *Im Lauf der Zeit* (1976) is literally translated as *In the Course of Time,* but the title of the film as released for American distribution is *Kings of the Road.*

The best strategy is to use both titles when you first refer to the movie: *Im Lauf der Zeit (Kings of the Road).* Then, throughout the rest of the essay, use one version consistently.

Checking these titles can not only result in a more accurate and professional paper, but sometimes, as in the last example, suggest central themes that are lost in the translation. Indeed, with some movies, the history of a title change may be the beginning of the essay itself:

> Ivan Passer's *Cutter's Way* (1981) went through several title changes before it achieved its modest success, and the history of those changes is, at the very least, an interesting example of American distribution strategies.

Foreign Words and Quotation Marks

Perhaps because of its international mobility and scope, film has attracted a large number of terms and expressions from other languages, especially French. Terms like *montage, cinema vérité,* and *mise-en-scène* have become a standard part of the film vocabulary in English and can be found in many recent English dictionaries. Accordingly, they do not necessarily need to be underlined or placed in quotation marks. For instances in which less familiar terms are borrowed from a foreign language, such as the Japanese *benshi,* which refers to the person who narrated silent movies in that country, these words should be underlined or italicized.

If you are quoting dialogue or commentary in a foreign language, do not underline it. If there is any doubt about whether your reader or readers know that language, you should append a translation in parentheses or in a footnote.

Sexist Language

When you are referring to a person or persons whose gender is unspecified, it can be offensive to use a masculine pronoun ("Watching this movie, a modern spectator sees his world from a very different angle"). It is preferable to double or split those pronouns ("his or her," "s/he"). Because this wording is awkward, however, it may be better yet to solve the problem by using the plural ("Watching this movie, modern spectators see their world from a very different angle") or by eliminating the possessive ("Watching this movie, a modern spectator sees the world from a very different angle"). When a gender difference involves nouns, a writer may use words that are not gender specific: Instead of *man* or *mankind*, use *person, individual*, or *people*.

Spelling

Misspelling a director's name or the title of a film under discussion is a good way to undermine your paper from the beginning, because it implies a careless attitude toward the whole project. The spelling of certain words—for example, *parallel, separate, subtly, symmetry*, and *prominent*—is traditionally a problem for many writers. All of us have our own list of problem words that demand watching. Unhappily, there are no easy or formulaic solutions for those who have difficulty with spelling, except perhaps being alert and attentive to it: A good writer always has a dictionary nearby and uses it. Even if you use a "spell-check" program with your word processor, double-check the spelling when you've printed out your hard copy.

LAST WORDS

In those moments of inevitable frustration, recall the words of Racine: "My tragedy is finished. All that is left to do is to write it."

Suggestions for Further Readings

For the student continuing in film studies, the following is a selective list of textbooks and anthologies that more fully examine and develop the tools and vocabulary for film analysis.

Introductory texts with detailed and extensive discussions of the formal features of films and the industrial and technological forces behind them:

Barsam, Richard, and Dave Monahan. *Looking at Movies: An Introduction to Film.* 3rd ed. New York: Norton, 2010.

Bordwell, David, and Kristin Thompson. *Film Art: An Introduction.* 9th ed. New York: McGraw-Hill, 2010.

Corrigan, Timothy, and Patricia White. *The Film Experience: An Introduction.* 2nd ed. Boston: Bedford/St. Martin's, 2009.

Monaco, James. *How to Read a Film: Movies, Media, and Beyond.* 4th ed. New York: Oxford University Press, 2009.

Pramaggiore, Maria, and Tom Wallis. *Film: A Critical Introduction.* 2nd ed. Boston: Pearson, 2007.

History textbooks that present the specific films, movements, and individuals shaping world cinemas from 1895 to the present:

Bordwell, David, and Kristin Thompson. *Film History: An Introduction.* 3rd ed. New York: McGraw-Hill, 2009.

Cook, David. *A History of Narrative Film.* 4th ed. New York: Norton, 2004.

Kawin, Bruce, and Gerald Mast. *A Short History of the Movies.* 9th ed. New York: Longman, 2006.

Nowell-Smith, Geoffrey, ed. *The Oxford History of World Cinema.* New York: Oxford University Press, 1999.

Anthologies that gather the most important essays in classic and contemporary film and media theory:

Braudy, Leo, and Marshall Cohen, eds. *Film Theory and Criticism.* 7th ed. New York: Oxford University Press, 2009.

Corrigan, Timothy, and Patricia White, with Meta Mazaj, eds. *Critical Visions in Film Theory: Classic and Contemporary Readings.*

Stam, Robert, and Toby Miller. *Film and Theory: An Anthology.* Malden, Mass.: Blackwell, 2000.

Appendix

SYMBOLS COMMONLY USED IN MARKING PAPERS

All instructors have their own techniques for annotating essays, but many instructors use the following symbols:

ab	faulty or undesirable abbreviation	*l*	logic; this does not follow
agr	faulty agreement between subject and verb or between pronoun and antecedent	*lc*	use lower case, not a capital
		mar	margins
		mm	misplaced or dangling modifier
apos	apostrophe		
awk(k)	awkward	¶	new paragraph
cap	use a capital letter	*paral*	faulty parallel, or use a parallel here
cf	comma fault		
choppy	too many short sentences; subordinate	*pass*	weak use of the passive
cl	cliché	*ref*	reference of pronoun vague or misleading
coh	paragraph lacks coherence, sentence lacks coherence	*rep*	undesirable repetition
		run	run-on sentence
cs	comma splice	*source*	give your source
dev	paragraph poorly developed	*sp*	misspelling
		sub	subordinate
dm	dangling modifier	*t*	tense incorrect
emph	emphasis unclear	*trans*	transition needed
frag	fragmentary sentence	*u*	lack of unity
good	a good point, or well expressed	*usage*	faulty usage
		wdy	wordy
id	unidiomatic expression	*ww*	wrong word
		X	This is wrong.
ital	underline to indicate italics	?	Really? Are you sure? I doubt it, or I can't read your writing.
k (awk)	awkward		

173

Glossary of Film Terms

aerial shot A shot from high above, usually from a crane or helicopter.

angle The position of the camera or point of view in relation to the subject being shown. Seen from above, the subject would be shot from a "high angle"; from below, it would be depicted from a "low angle."

animation A method used to make inanimate figures or objects come to life on the screen. This can be done by drawing on individual frames or by photographing an object one frame at a time while slightly changing the position of the object.

aspect ratio The ratio of the width to the height of the film image. The traditional "academic ratio" is 1.33:1. Since the 1950s, wide-screen ratios have become the norm, ranging from 1.66:1 to 2.55:1.

asynchronous sound Sound that does not have its source in the film image.

backlighting Light that comes from behind the person or object being filmed, often creating a silhouette around that subject.

chiaroscuro lighting The composition of light and dark in an image or picture.

cinematography The technical term for the various stages of motion-picture photography, from the manipulation of the film in the camera to the printing of that film.

close-up An image in which the distance between the subject and the point of view is very short, as in a "close-up of a person's face."

composition The arrangement and relationship of the visual elements within a frame.

computer graphics Images created electronically by a computer, often used for special effects or to manipulate photographic images.

continuity editing An editing style that follows a linear and chronological movement forward, as if the image is simply recording the action. Because it creates the illusion of reality, it is often called *invisible editing*.

contrapuntal sound Sound that counterpoints or contrasts the image.

crane shot An image depicting the subject from overhead, usually with the camera mounted on a mechanical crane.

crosscutting An editing technique that alternates between two different actions or scenes.

cutting Changing from one image to another; a version of this linkage is sometimes referred to as *montage*.

depth of field A range of planes within an image from foreground to background, all of which are in focus.

direct sound Sound recorded at the same time as the image is filmed.

dissolve An editing transition whereby one image fades out while another fades in.

documentary A nonfiction film about real events and people, often avoiding traditional narrative structures.

dubbing The recording of dialogue or other sound effects during the editing of a film.

DVD technology The recording and playing of films as "digital video discs," which can be viewed on DVD players or, increasingly, on computer drives. Besides the potential for higher-quality sound and images, DVDs allow for manipulation of the image, such as screen format, and can offer supplemental materials, such as interviews with the stars.

eyeline match The editing or joining of different shots by following the logic and direction of a character's glance or look.

fade-in An editing transition whereby an image gradually appears on a blackened screen.

fade-out An editing transition whereby an image gradually disappears onto a blackened screen.

fast motion When action is filmed at less than twenty-four frames per second, the projection of that action at twenty-four frames per second will appear to move at a more rapid than normal pace.

feature The main attraction when a group of films are shown. It can also refer to any film from 90 to 120 minutes long shown exclusively at a theater.

fill light Supplemental lighting that fills in or accentuates the key lighting on a filmed subject.

film gauge The width of film stock measured in millimeters, ranging from 8 mm (for home movies) to 70 mm (for commercial blockbusters).

filmography A list of films with information that ranges from just the title to complete details about the film, such as director, producer, running time, and so forth.

flashback An image, scene, or sequence that appears in a narrative to describe a past action or event.

flashforward An image, scene, or sequence that appears in a narrative to describe a future action or event.

focus The clarity and detail of an image, produced by the type of lens used and the distance between the camera and the object being filmed.

formalism A critical perspective that attends mainly to the structure and style of a movie or group of movies.

frame The borders of the image within which the subject is composed.

freeze frame When the movement of the film image appears to stop so that it appears like a photographic still.

full shot A shot that shows the whole body of the individual being filmed.

genre A critical category for organizing films according to shared themes, styles, and narrative structures; examples are "horror films" and "gangster films."

handheld shot A shot filmed from the shoulder of a cameraperson, usually creating the subjective perspective of an individual.

highlighting Sharp or intense lighting used to concentrate or highlight a detail of a person or object.

ideology An analytical approach that attempts to unmask the stated or unstated social and personal values that inform a movie or group of movies.

intertitles Mostly associated with silent film, images that present printed information or dialogue about the images before or after the intertitle.

iris shot The expansion or contraction of a small circle within the darkened frame to open or close a shot or scene.

jump cut A cut within the continuous action of a shot, creating a spatial or temporal jump or discontinuity within the action.

key lighting The central source of artificial light on a scene or subject. High-key scenes are entirely lit by this source; low-key scenes have very little artificial lighting.

long shot An image in which the distance between the camera and the subject is great.

match cut An edit that links two shots by a continuous sound or action.

medium close-up A shot that shows an individual from the torso to the head.

medium long shot A shot that reveals the entire body of a person or object along with a large part of the surrounding scene.

medium shot A shot that shows an individual from the waist up.

mirror shot A shot that reveals a person or scene through its reflection in a mirror.

mise-en-scène The arrangement of the so-called theatrical elements before they are actually filmed; these include sets, lighting, costumes, and props.

model shot A shot that uses small constructions or miniatures to create the illusion of real objects.

montage A specific kind of editing in which objects and figures are linked in a variety of creative or unexpected ways. Usually this kind of editing aims to generate certain effects or ideas.

narrative The way a story is constructed through a particular point of view and arrangement of events.

off-screen space Areas that are not shown by the image but sometimes suggested by actions or words within the image.

180-degree system A traditional rule for filming action so that the camera does not cross an imaginary 180-degree line. It is meant to create a stable spatial orientation for all action filmed.

pan A shot that pivots from left to right or right to left without the camera changing its position.

parallel action Two or more actions that are linked by the film to appear simultaneous.

point of view The position from which an action or subject is seen, often determining its significance.

process shot A shot that employs special effects during or after the filming of the shot.

rack focus A quick change of focus within a shot so that one object appears suddenly out of focus and another appears suddenly in focus.

reaction shot A shot that cuts from an object, person, or action to show another person or persons' reaction.

resolution The degree of sharpness in an image.

scene A space within which a narrative action takes place; it is composed of one or more shots.

score The musical sound track for a movie.

screenplay The literary description of film that may be a description of characters, dialogue, and actions or may contain exact shots and scenes.

sequence A series of scenes or shots unified by a shared action or motif.

set The place or location used for a specific scene or shot in a film.

shallow focus A shot in which only objects and persons in the foreground of the image can be seen clearly.

shot A continuously exposed and unedited image of any length.

shot/reverse shot An editing pattern that cuts between individuals according to the logic of their conversation.

slow motion When action is filmed at a speed faster than twenty-four frames a second, that action appears unusually slow when projected at normal speed.

soft focus By using filters (or even Vaseline) on the camera lens, objects and individuals will appear blurred or with hazy definition.

sound effects Any number of uses of sound other than music or dialogue.

sound track Using either optical or magnetic recording technology, the dimension of the film that includes music, noise, dialogue, and any other aural effects.

special effects A term used to describe a range of technological additions to the film to manipulate or alter what has been filmed.

subjective camera A technique that recreates the perspective of a single individual.

subtitle Printed titles, usually at the bottom of the film frame, that add descriptions to the image or translate the dialogue from one language to another.

swish pan A pan shot that moves rapidly from right to left or left to right, creating a blurring effect.

synchronous sound Sound whose source is identified by the film image.

take The recording of an image on film, usually used in writing as a temporal measure, such as a "long take" or a "short take."

tilt shot A shot that moves vertically up or down without changing the position of the camera.

tracking shot The movement of the image through a scene, photographed by a camera mounted on tracks. A dolly shot creates the same movement with a camera mounted on a mechanical cart, while a handheld camera is mounted on a cameraperson's shoulder.

videotape Magnetic tape used to record films for distribution and playing on VCR machines. The quality of both the film sound and image usually deteriorate on videotape.

voice-over The voice of someone, not seen in the narrative image, who describes or comments on that image.

wide-screen An aspect ratio that exceeds the traditional 1.33:1 ratio of width to height. The most common widescreen ratios are 1.66:1 and 1.85:1.

wipe An editing technique whereby a line crossing (or "wiping") one image replaces it with another image.

zoom shot The movement of the image according to focal adjustments of the lens, without the camera being moved.

Works Cited

Allen, Robert, and Douglas Gomery. *Film History: Theory and Practice.*
New York: Knopf, 1985.

Altman, Rick. "The Evolution of Sound Technology." *Film Sound: Theory
and Practice.* Ed. Elisabeth Weiss and John Belton. New York: Columbia
University Press, 1985. 44–53.

Barr, Charles. "Cinemascope: Before and After." *Film Quarterly* 16.4 (1963):
4–25.

Barsam, Richard Meran. "Leni Riefenstahl: Artifice and Truth in a World
Apart." *Film Comment* 9 (1973): 32–37.

Beckman, Karen. *Vanishing Women: Magic, Film, and Feminism.* Durham,
N.C.: Duke University Press, 2003.

Berger, John. *Ways of Seeing.* New York: Penguin, 1977.

Bordwell, David, and Kristin Thompson. *Film Art: An Introduction.* 2nd ed.
New York: Knopf, 1986.

Burch, Noël. *Theory of Film Practice.* Princeton, N.J.: Princeton University
Press, 1969.

———. *To the Distant Observer: Form and Meaning in Japanese Cinema.* Ed.
Annette Michelson. Berkeley and Los Angeles: University of California
Press, 1979.

Canby, Vincent. "The Screen: *Badlands* Is Ferociously American." *New York
Times,* March 24, 1974: 40.

Clair, René. "How Films Are Made." *Film: An Anthology.* Ed. Dan Talbot.
Berkeley: University of California Press, 1959. 225–33.

———. "The Art of Sound." *Film Sound: Theory and Sound.* Ed. Elisabeth Weiss
and John Belton. New York: Columbia University Press, 1985. 92–95.

Cocteau, Jean. "Cocteau on the Film." *Film: A Montage of Theories.* Ed.
Richard Dyer MacCann. New York: Dutton, 1966. 216–24.

Cook, David. *A History of Narrative Film.* New York: Norton, 1981.

Cook, Pam. "*The Gold Diggers.*" *Framework* 24 (1981): 27.

De Quincey, Thomas. "On the Knocking at the Gate in *Macbeth.*" *De Quincey's
Collected Writings.* Vol. 10. Ed. David Masson. Edinburgh: Adam and
Charles Black, 1890. 389–94.

Elsaesser, Thomas. "*Shock Corridor* by Samuel Fuller." *Movies and Methods.*
Vol. 1. Ed. Bill Nichols. Berkeley: University of California Press, 1976.
290–96.

Gunning, Tom. "*A Trip to the Moon.*" *Film Analysis.* Ed. Jeffrey Geiger and R. L. Rutsky. New York: Norton, 2005. 64–80.

Henderson, Brian. "Exploring *Badlands.*" *Wide Angle* 5.4 (1983): 38–55.

Hess, John. "*Godfather II:* A Deal Coppola Couldn't Refuse." *Jump Cut* 7 (1975): 10–11.

Langer, Susanne. *Feeling and Form.* New York: Scribner's, 1953.

Mast, Gerald. *Howard Hawks: Storyteller.* New York: Oxford University Press, 1982.

Monaco, James. *How to Read a Film.* New York: Oxford University Press, 1981.

Naremore, James. *Acting in the Cinema.* Berkeley: University of California Press, 1988.

Nowell-Smith, Geoffrey. "Shape and a Black Point." *Sight & Sound* 33.1. [Quoted from *Movies and Methods.* Vol. 1. Ed. Bill Nichols. Berkeley: University of California Press, 1976. 354–62.]

Panofsky, Erwin. "Style and Medium in the Motion Pictures." *Film Theory and Criticism.* 4th ed. Ed. Gerald Mast et al. New York: Oxford University Press, 1992. 233–48.

Sarris, Andrew. "Stranded in Soho's Mean Streets." *The Village Voice,* September 17, 1985: 54.

Schrader, Paul. *Transcendental Style in Film: Ozu, Bresson, Dreyer.* Berkeley: University of California Press, 1972.

Sklar, Robert. *Movie-Made America: A Cultural History of American Movies.* New York: Vintage, 1975.

Smith, Paul Julian. "*Chaotic Ana.*" *Film Quarterly* 61.2 (Winter 2007): 30–34.

Sobchack, Vivian. "Lounge Time: Postwar Crises and the Chronotrope of Film Noir." *Refiguring American Film Genres.* Ed. Nick Browne. Berkeley: University of California Press, 1998. 129–70.

Spoto, Donald. *The Art of Alfred Hitchcock.* New York: Doubleday, 1976.

Tolstoy, Leo. "It May Turn Out to Be a Powerful Thing." *Kino: A History of Russian and Soviet Film.* Ed. Jay Leyda. London: Allen and Unwin, 1960. 410–11.

Truffaut, François. "We Must Continue Making Progress." *Film: A Montage of Theories.* Ed. Richard Dyer MacCann. New York: Dutton, 1966. 368–76.

Ukadike, N. Frank. "African Cinema." *The Oxford Guide to Film Studies.* Ed. John Hill and Church Gibson. New York: Oxford University Press, 1998. 569–77.

Vogel, Amos. "On Seeing a Mirage." *Film Comment* 17.1 (1981): 76–78.

Warshow, Robert. *The Immediate Experience.* New York: Atheneum, 1975.

Williams, Christopher, ed. *Realism and Cinema.* London: Routledge, 1980.

Wood, Robin. "Sam Peckinpah." *Cinema: A Critical Dictionary.* Vol. 2. Ed. Richard Roud. London: Martin Secker and Warburg, 1980. 771–75.

Photo Credits

Frontispiece: Courtesy of Mary Evans/ Everett Collection

Page 3: ©*20th Century Fox*/Everett Collection

Page 11: *Badlands.* Author's Collection.

Page 19: *Utamaro and His Five Women.* Author's Collection.

Pages 29–33: *The Battleship Potemkin.* Author's Collection.

Page 34: *The Marriage of Maria Braun.* Author's Collection.

Page 38: *The Conformist.* Author's Collection.

Page 41: *Casablanca.* Author's Collection.

Page 44: ©*Sony Pictures Classics*/ Everett Collection

Page 45: *Full Metal Jacket.* The Kobal Collection/Warner Bros.

Page 47: *Rear Window.* Author's Collection.

Page 52: *DreamWorks*/Photofest

Page 53: ©*Twentieth Century Fox Film Corporation*/Everett Collection

Page 55: *Close Encounters of the Third Kind.* Author's Collection.

Page 61: *The Exorcist.* Author's Collection.

Pages 74–75: *The Thirty-Nine Steps.* Author's Collection.

Page 87: *Xala.* Author's Collection.

Page 95: ©*Fox Searchlight*/Everett Collection

Pages 97–98: *M. Courtesy*/The Everett Collection.

Page 110: *The Weinstein Company*/Photofest

Page 127: *Mishima.* Author's Collection.

Page 149: *Bonnie and Clyde.* Author's Collection.

Index